THE HEART OF ENGLAND

THE HEART OF ENGLAND

By Edward Thomas

faber and faber

This edition first published in 2008
by Faber and Faber Ltd
3 Queen Square, London WC1N 3AU

A CIP record for this book is available from the British Library

ISBN 978-0-571-24296-2

NOTE

Of the five songs printed at the end of this book, only "La Fille du Roi" has been published before, I believe. "The Holm Bank Hunting Song" and "Poor Old Horse" were sung by competitors for folk-song prizes at the annual Westmoreland Musical Festival, and I owe them to the kindness of Mr. George Rathbone. "The Mowing Song" and "Mary, come into, the Field," were given to me by friends.

EDWARD THOMAS.

CONTENTS

PART I
LEAVING TOWN

PART II
THE LOWLAND

PART III

THE UPLAND

PART IV

THE MOUNTAINS

PART V

THE SEA

PART I

LEAVING TOWN

CHAPTER I

LEAVING TOWN

SUNDAY afternoon had perfected the silence of the suburban street. Every one had gone into his house to tea; none had yet started for church or promenade; the street was empty, except for a white pigeon that pecked idly in the middle of the road and once leaned upon one wing, raised the other so as to expose her tender side and took the rain deliciously; so calm and unmolested was the hour.

The houses were in unbroken rows and arranged in pairs, of which one had a bay window on the ground floor and one had not. Some had laurels in front; some had names. But they were so much alike that the street resembled a great storehouse where yards of goods, all of one pattern, are exposed, all with that painful lack of character that makes us wish to rescue one and take it away and wear it, and soil it, and humanize it rapidly.

Soon a boy of nine years old came out of one house and stood at the gate. At first he moved briskly and looked in every direction as if expecting to see someone whom he knew; but in a little while he paused and merely looked towards the pigeon, so fixedly that perhaps he saw it not. The calm silenced him, took him into its bosom, yet also depressed him. Had he dared, he would have shouted or run; he would have welcomed the sound of a piano, of a dog barking, of a starling coldly piping. While he still paused an

old man rounded the corner of the street and came
down in the roadway towards him.

The old man was small and straight, and to his
thin figure the remains of a long black coat and grey
trousers adhered with singular grace. You could not
say that he was well dressed, but rather that he was
in the penultimate stage of a transformation like
Dryope's or Daphne's, which his pale face had not
altogether escaped. His neglected body seemed to have
grown this grey rind that flapped like birch bark. Had
he been born in it the clothing could not have been
more apt. The eye travelled from these clothes with
perfect satisfaction—as from a branch to its fruit—to
his little crumpled face and its partial crust of hair.
Yet he walked. One hand on a stick, the other
beneath a basket of watercress, he walked with quick,
short steps, now and then calling out unexpectedly, as
if in answer to a question, "Watercresses!" No one
interrupted him. He was hungry; he nibbled at
pieces of cress with his gums, and so kneaded his
face as if it had been dough. He passed the boy;
he stooped, picked up a rotten apple, and in the act
frightened the pigeon, which rose, as the boy saw,
and disappeared.

The boy raised his head and watched. He saw the
old man—as in an eloquent book and not with his
own usually indolent eyes—and thought him a traveller.
Yes! that was how a traveller looked—a strange, free
man, hatless, walking in the road, ignoring puddles,
talking carelessly to himself; from the country—such
was his stick and the manner of his clothes; with
something magnificent and comely in his hoariness;
sleeping the boy knew not where, perhaps not at all,
but going on and on, certainly not to church, but

perhaps to places with mountains, icebergs, houses in the branches of trees, great waters, camels, monkeys, crocodiles, parrots, ivory, cannibals, curved swords. And the boy flushed to think that the quiet street was an avenue to all the East, the Pole, the Amazon . . . to dark men who wondered about the sunlight, the wind, the rain, and whence they came . . . to towns set down in the heart of forests and lonely as ships at sea. But whatever he was, the old man was more blessed than any one whom the boy had ever seen.

The old man was gone out of sight. The boy started to run and follow; but he stumbled and fell and uttered his intolerable longing in a fir of grave tears, while the street began to be bright and restless again.

I thought to follow him myself. But the next day I was still in that grey land, looking at it from a railway train.

The hundreds of streets parallel or at angles with the railway — some exposing flowery or neglected back gardens, bedrooms half seen through open windows, pigeon houses with pigeons bowing or flashing in flight, all manner of domesticities surprised — others a line of shop fronts and gorgeous or neat or faded women going to and fro — others, again, a small space that had been green and was still grassy under its encumbrance of dead trees, scaffolding, and bricks — some with inns having good names — these streets are the strangest thing in the world. They have never been discovered. They cannot be classified. There is no tradition about them. Poets have not shown how we are to regard them. They are to us as mountains were in the Middle Ages, sublime, difficult, immense;

and yet so new that we have inherited no certain attitude towards them, of liking or dislike. They suggest so much that they mean nothing at all. The eye strains at them as at Russian characters which are known to stand for something beautiful or terrible; but there is no translator: it sees a thousand things which at the moment of seeing are significant, but they obliterate one another. More than battlefield or library, they are dense with human life. They are as multitudinous and painful and unsatisfying as the stars. They propose themselves as a problem to the mind, only a little less so at night when their surfaces hand the mind on to the analogies of sea waves or large woods.

Nor at the end of my journey was the problem solved. It was a land of new streets and half-built streets and devastated lanes. Ivied elm trunks lay about with scaffold poles, uprooted shrubs were mingled with bricks, mortar with turf, shining baths and sinks and rusty fire grates with dead thistles and thorns. Here and there a man in a silk hat or a little girl with neat ankles and high brown boots stepped amidst the deeply rutted mud. An artist who wished to depict the Fall, and some sympathy with it in the face of a ruined Eden, might have had little to do but copy an acre of the surviving fields.

A north wind swept the land clean. In the hedges and standing trees, it sobbed at intervals like a bitter child forcing himself to cry; in the windowless houses it made a merrier sound like a horn. It drove workmen and passers-by to spend as much time as possible in "The King's Head," and there the medley of the land was repeated. Irish and Cockney accents mingled with Kentish; American would not have been out of place.

No one seemed to dislike the best room in the inn, where there was a piano, a coloured picture of Lord Roberts and of the landlord as a youth, an old print of snipe-shooting, some gaudy and fanciful advertisements of spirits, and no fire to warm the wall-paper which had once had a pattern characteristic of poor bathrooms.

I felt a kind of exalted and almost cheerful gloom as I stepped out and saw that it was raining and would go on raining. O exultation of the sorrowful heart when Nature also seems to be sorrowing.' What strange merriment is this which the dejected mind and the wind in the trees are making together! What high lavolt of the shuffling heels of despair! As two lovers wounded and derided will make of their complainings one true joy that triumphs, so will the concealing rain and the painful mind.

The workmen had gone; faint lights began to appear through the blinds of the finished houses. There was no sunset, no change from day to night. The end of the day was like what is called a natural death in bed; an ill-laid fire dies thus. With the darkness a strange spirit of quiet joy appeared in the air. Old melodies floated about it on that mourning wind. The rain formed a mist and a veil over the skeletons round about, but it revealed more than it took away; Nature gained courage in the gloom. The rain soothed her as it will wash away tears on the lonely hills. The trees were back in Eden again. They were as before in their dim, stately companies. The bad walking was no annoyance. Once I came upon a line of willows above dead reeds that used to stand out by a pond as the first notice to one walking out of London that he was in the country at last; they were unchanged; they welcomed and encouraged once more. The lighted windows in the mist had each a greeting; they were as the windows we strain our eyes for as we descend to them from the hills of Wales or Kent; like those, they had the art of seeming a magical encampment among the trees, brave, cheerful lights which men and women kept going amidst the dense and powerful darkness. The thin, incompleted walls learned a venerable utterance.

The night grew darker. The sound of pianos mingled with the wind. I could not see the trees— I was entrapped in a town where I had once known nothing but fields and one old house, stately and reticent among the limes. A sense of multitude surged about and over me—of multitudes entirely unknown to me—collected by chance—mere numbers—human faces that were at that moment expressing innumerable strange meanings with which I had nothing to do. Had I said to one who entered an adjacent house that I was retrospectively a lodger of his, since I had once hidden for half a day in the hollow oak in his front garden, he would have stared. Here were people living in no ancient way. That they supped and slept in their houses was all that was clear to me. I wondered why—why did they go on doing these things? Did they ever sit up thinking and thinking, trying to explain to themselves why they were there, and then fall asleep in their chairs and awake still with the same goalless thought and so go shivering to bed? The window lights were now as strange to me and as fascinating as, to a salmon swaying by a bridge, the lights and faces of the poachers on the bank. As if it were new came back to me the truism that most men are prisons to themselves. Here was a city imprisoned deep, and I as deep, in the rain. Was there, perhaps, joy somewhere on account of those thousands of prisoners and lighted windows?

I left London that night on foot. By way of preparation, I stayed until after midnight to listen to a sweet voice that drew upon all the gloom and jangle of London the sweet patterns of some old country melodies. Strange and pleasant it was to look out upon the London night of angry-ridged, tumultuous roofs, and then, sharply drawing a curtain, to live upon a cadence, a melody —

> As I walked forth one Midsummer morning
> A-viewing the meadows and to take the air . . .

A pure rose upon a battlefield, a bright vermeil shell upon a slatternly sea-shore after storm, would not be of a more piercing beauty than those songs just there.

Then I set out and began to stain the immense silence of the city with the noise of my heels and stick. A journalist or two went by; a fat man and his fat dog straying from the neat bar of a Conservative Club homewards without precipitancy; a few pleasure-seekers with bleared or meditative eye; a youth with music in his steps, fresh from some long evening of talk and song, perhaps his first. Here was a policéman stern and expectant in a dark entry, or smoking a pipe; there stood, or sat or leaned or lay, men and women who no more give, up their secrets than the blinded windows and the doors that will not be knocked at for hours yet. How noble the long, well-lighted streets at this hour, fit with their smooth paved ways for some roaring game, and melancholy because there is no one playing. The rise and fall of the land is only now apparent. In the day we learn of hills

in London only by their fatigue; in the night we can
see them as if the streets did not exist, as they must
have appeared to men who climb them with a hope
of seeing their homes from the summits or of surprising a stag beneath. The river ran by, grim, dark,
and vast, and having been untouched by history, old
as hills and stars, it seemed from a bridge, not like
a wild beast in a pit, but like a strange, reminiscential
amulet, worn by the city to remind her that she shall
pass. How tameless and cold the water, alien, careless,
monstrous, capable of drowning in a little while the
uttermost agony or joy and making them as if they
had never been. I passed by doors where lived people
whom I knew, but it was two o'clock in the morning;
they could not know me. I wondered which of them
I could safely disturb. With what expression would
they come down from their warm beds and oblivion,
with dull, puzzled eyes, and slowly recall those things
which—even the pleasant ones—our lonely lives so
often reduce to mere entries in a tedious chronicle.
I left the question unanswered.

Now I saw a tall, stiff crane surmounting the houses
and nodding in the sky, itself simple, strong, direct,
weighing the city against the heavens in an enormous
balance with Rhadamanthine solemnity.

Endless were the vast caves and deserts of the streets,
most strange the unobserved, innumerable things prepared for the eyes of men on the coming day—
glittering windows of cutlery, food, drugs, saddlery—
the high walls with coloured advertisements of beer,
medicine, food, actors, newspapers, corsets, concerts,
pickles. The dark windows, the windows lit to serve
some purpose unknown, seemed to make it necessary
to cry out, to raise an alarm, to make sure that the

darkness or light meant only the usual things. Now and then several streets ran towards one another and left a square or irregular space at their meeting, surrounded by an inn with a sign, a stone trough, an old eighteenth-century house, its windows emphasized by white paint, a row of pollarded limes, a scrap of orchard—once perhaps the heart of a village. Or for almost a mile the streets ran straight, with branches at right angles, and suddenly a large house stood back and its garden of limes and lawn broke the monotone. The names of the streets were an epitome of the world and time, commemorating famous and unknown men, battles, conspiracies, far-off cities and rivers, little villages known to me, streams and hills now buried by houses; the names of the inns were as rich as the titles of books in an old library, suggested many an inn by wood and mill and meadow and village square, but all confused as if in a marine store. And as I walked through old and new villages, rents, courts, alleys, lanes, rises, streets, buildings, roads, avenues, I seemed to be travelling through the Inferno and Purgatorio, but before the first man had entered them and without a guide. It was immense, sublime, but its purposes dark and not to be explained by the policemen here and there in charge. Nor, passing through Battersea, did I meet the famous man who has threaded this mystery. He, at least, would have taken me to a housetop and have unravelled space; but I expected him at street corners and on commons in vain. But presently I reached a sign-post that stood boldly up with undoubted inscriptions, one of them to London, and away from that I set my face, though I saw market-carts going the way I had come, with drowsy carters, one lamp, and horses whose shadowy muscles quivered in the electric light. That sign-post seemed to make all things clear. Like a prophet it rose up, who after an age of darkness says that the path of life and goodness is plain, that he knows it, and that all who follow him will be saved. Not for him hesitation and qualification; but to all men perplexed by definitions, testimonies, other prophets and their own thoughts, he cries: "This is the way."

The world may find the Spring by following her.

I followed and needed only a good marching song. By chance I lighted on one which was first sung by countrymen. It is not triumphant—the mind wearies of a triumphant song in solitude and at night—but it persists and acknowledges no end. It was made by feeble, mighty-limbed men who knew what it is to go on and on for ends which they do not entirely apprehend. It matches the hurrying feet of the lover or the limp of the hungry man at dawn. It begins:

With one man, with two men,
We mow the hay together;
With three men, with four men,
We mow the hay together;
With four, with three, with two, with one, no more,
We mow the hay and rake the hay and take it away together.

It goes on:

With five men, with six men,
We mow the hay together;
With seven men, with eight men,
We mow the hay together;
With eight, with seven, with six, with five, with four,
    with three, with two, with one, no more,
We mow the hay and rake the hay and take it away together.

It goes on until a hundred is reached, proceeding after

twenty by tens. And so, gradually, as the song went on, the houses opened apart, and the road ahead was a simple white line. On either hand thousands of lights showed valleys and hills; but ahead there was a promising darkness, and out of it came the Watercress Man with a basket of wild flowers on his back.

"Sir," said he, setting down his flowers slowly, "the price of a pint of ale won't hurt you, I suppose? I have drunk nothing since yesterday morning."

"But have you eaten anything?" I asked, ready to admire him for asking first for drink.

"No," said he, "I have neither eaten nor drunken. I drink four ale."

"Thank you," he said, when I had given him two-pence for drink and twopence for food. "We are all sons of one mother. You can't get away from that."

"Then we are brothers," said I.

"Certainly, if you will."

"I should like to know you."

"With pleasure, if you can."

"What are you by profession?"

"A hard question. I profess nothing. By conviction I am an ill-used man, and for the moment I am a seller of flowers."

He showed me his flowers—kingcups, cuckoo-flowers, primroses from the moist woods.

"I will buy your flowers," I said.

"No! I think I shall keep those," and he put them in a horse trough close by. I asked him if he would return into the country with me.

"No," he replied, "it would be sunrise before we got into the country, and I never spend the daytime in the country if I can avoid it."

"Why?" I asked.

"As we are brothers," he said, "I will tell you that I paint landscapes. I like nothing on earth so well as the country. I was dragged up in the Borough. The country for me! But the lover of Nature and the gamekeeper and the farmer and the landowner spoil it by day. The people are stupid, brutal. The women are not at all beautiful. Their cowsheds are the only things they have not spoilt: they are still sweet. As a lad I read the pastoral poets, and I know that these things were once far different. So I live in London and paint landscapes at sixpence apiece, sometimes four or five of them in a morning, so that I live well. I usually put a few red flowers in with the sixpennyworth. I am sixty-eight; my son will succeed me, but badly—badly."

"How is that?"

"Because he says that he paints Nature as she is, which is impossible. I make no such mistake, as you shall see—I aim for suggestion. Here," he said, producing one from his pocket (a brown field sloping up to a ridge of trees, painted black, against a silvery sky, and in that a few rooks). "Do you not hear there the wild, angry charm of hundreds of blackbirds and thrushes and larks? They sometimes make me lie down and cry before the sun rises, because I am not worthy; I do not own a little farm and drive my own plough and cause the envy of kings at my happiness."

"Is that clump of trees right?" I asked (in need of something to say).

"Right? But the feeling is there. Is it not cold and pure and wild? I felt great as I did that. But see here again!"

Here he brought out another, also in three colours, of a landscape at dawn. Three black firs stood at the top of a steep down, and from them went a pair of dark birds out along a silver sky.

"I never put figures in my landscapes," he explained, "but is not the spirit of a small sweet Amaryllis in it? *Ah! lovely as thou art to look upon, ah, heart of stone, ah, dark-browed maiden*! Does she not hide somewhere out of the picture; and does not a shepherd, seated perhaps under those fir trees, look for her coming? Is not the Golden Age in that sky?"

"I am glad," said I, "that you believe in a Golden Age. Literature and art are continually re-creating it for us."

"Modern literature," he said scornfully, "is by those who have not seen for those who do not care. What answer has literature to this?" Here he showed a third sketch.

"I know nothing of literature," I said; "I am a journalist."

He sighed with relief, and pointed to a yellow thatched house with windows open on to the sea, and behind the house the usual dark trees and silver sky.

"There," he exclaimed, "literature does not believe in or understand the honest life, bound up with the seasons and beauty which is expressed by that simple scene. See, there, equal laws, harmony, aims unspotted by the world, not fearing nor loving kings. Any thoughtful man living in a scene like that would be wiser, and it would be impossible for him to err. I myself would venture to be a Daphnis or Menalcas again there. I can hear the one living pastoral poet saying in that cottage by the sea:

> "Come, pretty Phyllis, you are late!
> The cows are crowding round the gate.

An hour or more, the sun has set;
The stars are out; the grass is wet;
The glow-worms shine; the beetles hum;
The moon is near—come, Phyllis, come!

The black cow thrusts her brass-tipped horns
Among the quick and bramble thorns;
The red cow jerks the padlock chain;
The dun cow shakes her bell again,
And round and round the chestnut tree
The white cow bellows lustily." . . .

He knew all four verses by heart.

"Your aims are wonderful," I stammered. "If I could only see you at work, if you would only show me the scenes which inspire such antique and lofty emotions . . ."

"See! this is London—nothing but trees—I have seen it so as I came home. But I cannot go with you. I return to think about the Golden Age."

He tied the flowers round the pole of a signboard that stood on a harsh courtyard of gravel strewn with dirty paper, and pursued his homeward road, eager for "The Old Angel" or "The Chequers" where he could vivify his vision of the Golden Age.

In the sky, the distant dawn sent up to the clouds a faint dream of light that made their shapes just visible. A hedge-sparrow awoke in the furze beside the road, twittered clearly and became silent again; on the other side, in some invisible trees high up, a few rooks began to talk. Then, for a little while as I went on, the darkness was complete, and the silence also, except that the telegraph wires forced a faint complaint out of the light wind.

As the clouds filled with that dream of light and the road began visibly to lengthen out, I left London behind or recognized it only in the blue bowls and copper-ware gleaming through the windows of new houses round about. Beyond them rolled a ploughed country of such abounding and processional curves that it seemed almost to move and certainly to rejoice; here and there the curves dimpled suddenly and made a hollow, where elm or beech sprang up in the midst of the ploughland, in a small consistory, grave, shining, fair. To right and left, where the curves of the land rose to the sky, the white foam of orchards half buried rosy farmhouses and their own dark boughs. The dense thorn hedges gleamed all wet, compelling the wind to dip deep into them and taste their fragrance, coolness, moistness, softness all together, envying not the earnest bee, or the dallying butterfly, or even the insect that was drowning in a dewy flower. How the dew washed away the night! I thought that the old man had spoken truly when he said that the Golden Age comes again with every dawn. The dew gave the eyes a kind of fitness and worthiness to behold the white fruit blossom and the sudden hills of horse-chestnut green. It washed out London as the old man's brush had done. See! the world is but a brown and fragrant cloud decorated with dark boles, green foliage, white bloom, and here and there a soul akin to them; it turns the wilful mind into a garden neat and fine, of red and white, with green lawns between, which the bee Fancy sucks at and combines. For a minute only, in one shadowed wood that faced the departing night, all the birds sang together stormily, and hardly moving from the sprays on which they slept, with something of night in their voices. But as I entered the wood, already the most of them had gone hither and thither, and only on

17

high twigs one or two blackbirds and thrushes sang, and hidden wood-pigeons cooed. The young hazel boughs bent at the top with fresh leaves that were so beautiful and frail that they seemed but just to have been persuaded to stay and give up a winged life. The low wych elm twigs had been dipped in leaves. Wild cherry leaves and flowers mingled like lovers so young that the boy rivals the girl in tenderness. There was no path, and pushing through hazel and cornel and thorn, I saw the eyes of sitting birds gleam with a little anger through the lustrous green. Presently the stems were less dense; a little river ran through freshly cut underwood of hazel and ash and oak, their wounds still flashing. There pale primroses and the last celandines ran in sharp gulfs into the heart of bluebell and orchis and cuckoo-flower, and the orange-tipped butterfly tripped over them. The mosses on the ash and hazel roots gleamed darkly gold and green. In the rivulet itself broad kingcups swayed and their leaves sank into darkness and rose into light as the ripples fluctuated. The blackbird, fed on golden hours, sang carelessly, time after time, the two opening phrases of an old Highland melody. Close by, in the cool, sombre, liquid air between the new-leaved boughs of beech sang a cuckoo, and his notes seemed not to die but to nestle and grow quiet among the leaves overhead and the flowers underfoot, and some of them even to find their embalming in the little round hawthorn clouds that sailed high above in a deep stream of blue.

Suddenly my mind went back to the high dark cliffs of Westminster Abbey, the blank doors and windows of endless streets, the devouring river, the cold gloom before dawn, and then with a shudder forgot them and saw the flowers and heard the birds with such a joy as when the ships from Tarshish, after three blank years, again unloaded apes and pea-cocks and ivory, and men upon the quay looked on; or as, when a man has mined in the dead desert for many days, he suddenly enters an old tomb, and making a light, sees before him vases of alabaster, furniture adorned with gold and blue enamel and the figures of gods, a chariot of gold, and a silence perfected through many ages in the company of death and of the desire of immortality.

PART II

THE LOWLAND

CHAPTER II

How nobly the ploughman and the plough and three horses, two chestnuts and a white leader, glide over the broad swelling field in the early morning! Under the dewy, dark-green woodside they wheel, pause, and go out into the strong light again, and they seem one and glorious, as if the all-breeding earth had just sent them up out of her womb—mighty, splendid, and something grim, with darkness and primitive forces clinging about them, and the night in the horses' manes.

The ship, the chariot, the plough, these three are, I suppose, the most sovereign beautiful things which man has made in his time, and such that were his race to pass away from the earth, would bring him most worship among his successors.

All are without parallel in nature, wrought out of his own brain by unaided man; and yet, during their life, worthy by their beauty, their purpose, and their motion to challenge anything made by the gods on the earth or in the sea; and after their life is done, sublime and full of awe, so that when we come upon them neglected and see their fair, heroic curves, the dirge at their downfall passes inevitably into a pæan to their majesty. And they are very old. Probably the beasts and the birds, the winds and waves and hills know us as the creatures who make the ship, the chariot, and the plough. These three things, as

23

they go about their work, must have become universal
symbols, so that when a man comes in sight, the
other inhabitants of the earth say: Here is he who
sails in ships and drives the chariot and guides the
plough. And the greatest of all is the plough. It is
without pride and also without vanity. The ship and
the chariot have sometimes tried to conceal their
ancient simplicity, though they have never done without it. But the plough is the same—in shape like
a running hound, with tail uplifted and muzzle
bowed to the scent.

Richard the ploughman is worthy of his plough and
team. He moves heavily with long strides over the
baked yellow field, swaying with the violent motion
of the plough as it cuts, the stubborn and knotty soil,
and yet seeming to sway out of joy and not necessity.
He is a straight, small-featured, thin-lipped man, red-
haired and with blue eyes of a fierce loneliness almost
fanatical. Hour after hour he crosses and recrosses
the field, up to the ridge, whence he can see miles
of hill and wood; down to the woodside where the
rabbits hardly trouble to hide as he appears, or to
the thick hedge with marigolds below and nearly all
day the song of nightingales. The furrow is always
straight; he could plough it so asleep, and sometimes
perhaps he does. The larks sing invisible in the white
May sky. The swallows and woodlarks and willow
wrens and linnets, with their tenderest of all mortal
voices, flit and sing about him. Partridges whirr and
twang. A fox steals along the hedge, a squirrel glows
and ripples across a bay of the field. And for a little
time he notices these things in a mild complacency.
He has even formed a theory that there is another
finch like a chaffinch, but not such a singer, and he

calls it a piefinch. He likes the bright weather, and his cheerful greeting leaves the passer-by feeling stupid because he cannot equal it; few sounds can equal it, except the shout of a cuckoo and the abandoned clamour of a deep-voiced hound. He never becomes tired; at noon and evening in the tavern, he drinks standing, with one hand on the high door latch and the other holding the tankard, and talking all the time at the rate of one phrase to a minute, with serious mouth and distant eyes which must be symbols to help out the words, for certainly if those words mean no more than they would in another man's mouth, they convey little but the apparent ennui of all those long hours walking to this oak or that hawthorn spray.

At first sight the ploughman's task seems to be one which ought rightly to be set only to some well-balanced philosopher, who could calmly descend into himself during the many lonely hours and think of nature and man in orderly thoughts. To the ordinary man, with his drug-habit of taking to reverie during any long spell of solitude, such a task would seem fatal. In fact, it is pretty certain that many a plain fellow must be turned into a fool by the immense monotony of similar furrows and the same view repeated exactly every quarter of an hour. When he is still a boy, he goes about, even in the four hours' darkness of the winter mornings, with always a song amidst the sleet or the silent frost. At lunch he can look for nests or nuts or hunt a stoat. When work is over he looks forward to songs at "The Chequers" with those of his own age, or to a shame-faced walk with a girl, or to fishing for tench and eels, or even to a game of cricket. But when he is married all that is past. He leads his horses down to the plough, having some simple thought, a grievance, a recollection, perhaps a hope, running confusedly in his head, and all day he turns it over, repeating himself, exaggerating, puzzling over the meaning of someone's words, floundering in digressions, fitting new words to the wood-pigeon's talk, trying to keep straight and to make up his mind, justifying himself, condemning another, cursing him. Now and then he lifts his eyes to the sky or the wooded hills and his mind catches at an impression which never becomes a thought, but something between a picture and a tune in the head, and its half-oblivion is pleasant, when suddenly the plough leaps forward from his relaxing grasp, he shouts "Ah, Charley!" to the leader, mutters a little, and settles down again to the grievance or the recollection or the hope, to be disturbed on lucky days by the hounds, perhaps, but otherwise to go on and on; and at noon and evening he takes his horses back to the stable and confronts men with the same simple ejaculations as before, after the last glass possibly reviving his lonely thoughts, but ineffectually. "How Bill does talk," they say. What wonder that the rustic moralist marks an infant's tomb with the words:

> When the archangel's trump shall blow
> And souls to bodies join,
> AMillions shall wish their lives belw
> Had been as brief as thine.

But Richard is no ordinary man, for he is happy and proud, and somewhere in the fields or in the clouds that roll before him as his plough comes to the top of the ridge, he has found that draught of excellent grace:

Few men but such as sober are and sage,
Are by the gods to drink thereof assigned;
But such as drink, eternal happiness do find.

There is little of wisdom in his words except moderation; but his garden is luckier, his kitchen sweeter than all the rest in the hamlet, and of all his tasks—ploughing, harrowing, rolling, drudging, reaping, mowing, carting faggots or corn or hay or green meat or dung—he likes none better than the others, because he likes them all well as they come. And ah! I to see him and his team all dark and large and heroic against the sky, ploughing in the winter or the summer morning, or to see him grooming the radiant horses in their dim stable on a calm, delaying evening, is to see one who is in league with sun and wind and rain to make odours fume richly from the ancient altar, to keep the earth going in beauty and fruitfulness for still more years.

CHAPTER III

NOT HERE, O APOLLO!

Iᴛ was a clay country of small fields that rose and fell slightly, not in curves, but in stiff lines which ended abruptly in the low, dividing hedges. Here and there we passed small woods of oak, hardly more than overgrown hedges, where keepers shot the jays. There were few streams—and those polluted. North and south the land rose up in some pomp to steep hills planted with oak and beech and fir, and between these, broad meadows and hop gardens, which now and then caught the faint light on their dry brown or moist green and gleamed desirably. The wind was in the north; it had rained in the night, and yet the morning was dull and the sun white and small. There was some vice in the wind or in the foliage or in the grass that now began to be long—some vice that made the land sad and cold and unawakening, with the surliness of a man who cannot sleep and will not rise.

The woods became more dense as we walked; not far ahead the oaks closed in and expounded the contours of the land by their summits. But our path led away from them, and we were about to lose sight of them when, gently as the alighting of a bird, the sunlight dropped among the tops of the oaks, which were yellow and purple with young leaves, and blessed them. We turned. There was the sun held fast among the fresh leaves and green trunks, as if Apollo had changed into a woodland god, and forsaken the long lonely ways of heaven, and resolved no more to spend a half of his days in the underworld. How the nymphs clapped their hands at this advent, abandoning Pan, and bringing to the new lord all choicest herbs and highest fair grasses and golden flowers that should make him content to be away from the clouds of sunset and dawn, and blue flowers on which his feet should tread without envy of. the infinite paths of the sky, and white flowers that should suffice for his shepherding in place of the flocks of the high desolate noon I How they drove up grey dove and green woodpecker to shake their wings and shine about the new god's head as they flew among the branches! How Pan himself, that does not heed dark hours, crept away from his light-hearted nymphs and hid in the sombre reeds! "Ever-young Apollo! Eternal Apollo! Young Apollo!" were the cries. "Why have we ever served a goat-foot god?" And so they made haste to serve him with the clearest honey of the wild bees, the cream from the farm that was most clean, the fruits that yet preserved flavours of a past summer and autumn in the granary close by, and fresh cresses from the spring; nor would some of the little satyrs forget the golden ale and amber bread and cheese of the colour of primroses; and all seemed assured that never again would Apollo forsake the red and yellow leaves of the full oaks or the mid-forest grasses or the lilied pools standing among willow and alder and ash. And we saw that the light was passing in triumph slowly, and accompanied by the cooing of doves, along the wood from oak top to oak top.

CHAPTER IV

WALKING WITH GOOD COMPANY

THE lightning grows upon the sky like a tumultuous thorn tree of fire. The thunder grumbles with interrupted cadences, and then, joyful as a poet, hits the long, grave, reverberating period at last, repeats it triumphantly, and muttering dies away. The pheasants in the woods have got over their alarm and have ceased to crow, and for a time the heavy perpendicular rain submerges the meadow and farmhouse and midfield oak and the steep downs with their cloudy woods; the birds are still.

Then the rain wastes away. I can count the drops on the broad burdock leaves; and the evening sun comes through horizontally; and it is good to be afoot and making for something remote, I know not why. Each meadow shines amid its encircling hedges like a lake of infinitely deep emerald. On the dark red ploughland the flints glitter with constellated or solitary lights. In the sweet copses, where the willow wren sings again in the highest branches, the thorn foliage is so bright that the dark stems are invisible. The purple oak tops reach wonderfully into the sombre, bluish sky, and over them the wood-pigeons turn rapidly from darkness to splendour—from splendour to darkness, as they wheel and clap their wings. The cuckoos shout again: first one, so far off that the character, without the notes, of the song is recognized; then another with a wild clearness in its voice as if the rainy air aided it; and then one just overhead, in the luminous grey branches of an oak, so that it can be heard trying hard and enjoying its own strength. The hills rejoice with long shadows and yellow light; the tall hares stretch themselves and gallop. The little pools hum pleasantly as the rain drips from their overhanging brier and bramble into the leaden water with bright splash. And in our own muscles and hearts the evening strives to form an aspiration that shall suit the joy of the hills, the meadows, the copses, and their people. We will go on, they say; we will go on and on, through the beeches on the hill and up over the ridge and down again through the grey wet meadows and to the old road between hawthorn and guelder-rose at the foot of the downs; and still on, not as before, but out of time and space, until we come—home—to some refuge of beauty and serenity in the heart of the immense evening. And so we will, though we shall be wise to find our achievement in the rapture of walking, or in the short rest upon a gate where we may surprise the twilight at her consecrating task. It is well, too, to talk, not to walk silently and weave such dreams as will make our host to-night intolerable; or if not to talk, then to sing some old song whose melody finds a strange fitness to our minds, in spite of the words, as for example:

> There's not a drunkard lives in our town
> Who is not glad that malt is gone down—
> > Malt is gone down, malt is gone down,
> > From an old angel to a French crown. . . .

Or,

> The fox jumped over the hedge so high. . . .

Or,

> Orientis partibus adventavit asinus. . . .

(Sung to the tune of the Welsh New Year's Eve Song)
Or,

There was a farmer's son kept sheep upon the hill,
And he went forth one May morning to see what he could kill,
Sing blow away the morning dew, the dew, and the dew,
Blow away the morning dew; how sweet the winds do blow. . . .

Or,

> Quand le marin revient de guerre—
> Tous doux—
> Quand le marin revient de guerre—
> Tous doux—
> "Tout mal chaussé, tout mal véto.
> Pauvre marin! d'ou reviens-tu?—
> Tous doux.,,

Then perhaps we will lazily inquire why songs about the price of malt, or the coming of a Beautiful Ass out of the East, should stir and uplift and compose the hearts of men dreaming of an ideal beauty on an April evening, and so to more songs and then to bed, finding at the last moment the serene and beautiful, perhaps, in the glimpse of holy evening landscape rich in unseen nightingales as we fall asleep.

CHAPTER V

FOR a mile, alongside a bright high road, runs a twelve-foot strip of grass and clover and buttercups, with cinquefoil's golden embroidery in the turf at the edge. Little circular heaps of silver wood ash mark the cold fires of tramps, here and there. Here also they sleep in the sun, in summer and autumn, and in winter lean in the dense hedge that keeps the north wind away. The hedge is rich and high, of thorn overgrown by traveller's joy and bryony; and at its feet, stitchwort, campions, vetchlings, and bird's-foot trefoil grow luxuriantly.

This is no man's garden. Every one who is nobody sits there with a special satisfaction, watching the swift, addle-faced motorist, the horseman, the farmer, the tradesman, the publican, go by; for here he is secure as in the grave, and even as there free—if he can—to laugh or scoff or wonder or weep at the world.

As I was trying to persuade some buoyant bryony strands with snaky heads to return to the hedge from which they had wandered into danger, a tramp came up.

"Have you seen my old woman?" he asked.

"Not know her? She is the cursedest, foulest-mouthed old woman in the country, fond of too much drink, and she has just been spending the winter in

33

prison—she prefers it to the workhouse which I have just left. But she just suits me. There is no one like her. They often tell me to take another instead of her, but I never will . . .

"I don't know that you would like to see her. She is not a beauty, and she is not dressed up well. She is as crooked as an oak branch, and she has one leg longer than the other, and as to her face I could make a better one myself with a handful of dirt. She drags as she walks, what with keeping up with me all these years. You may know her, because she is always smoking. She cannot eat; she lives on tobacco and beer . . .

"Oh, I see you are one of these antiquarian gents. If you would really like to see her . . .

"Well, if you are curious, how would you like to hear of the murder I did twenty years ago? I tell it to everybody, and they don't seem to believe me, so I will tell it to you . . .

"I spent a night in the workhouse and when I got out in the afternoon I was so hungry that I could have eaten the master, if he hadn't been the ugliest fellow I ever saw, like a fancy potato. Walking didn't cure my appetite, and all that day and night I didn't have a bite. Perhaps I got a bit queer and I went on walking until I got near to Binoll in Wiltshire where I was born. That is a fine country. My old woman and I have slept in violets there many a time in April. When I got there early in the morning on the second day I thought I would go into a copse I knew and pick some bluebells there, partly for old remembrance sake and partly to make a penny or two in Swindon, but I didn't much care what. Well, as I was picking them—God I how everything did smell and I felt like a little boy, I was enjoying it so, and putting my hand into all the nests and feeling the warm eggs—Lord! what a fool I be—I thought I would go to sleep. There was such a nice bit of moon in the sky, with the rim of the cup of it uppermost, which means that it keeps the rain from falling, but if it is upside down it lets the water out and you may know it will rain. There was a regular old-fashioned English thrush saying: 'Bit, bit, slingdirt, slingdirt, belcher, belcher, belcher,' and I went on picking the flowers. All of a sudden I saw two fellows sitting just outside the wood with their backs to me. One of them was a big fellow and we passed the time of day and he said he had done a job lately and was not in a hurry to do any more. The other was a little white-faced man such as I can't away with, and he said he was looking for a job and trying to get his strength up a bit. The big fellow motioned to me, meaning that the other had got money about him; so I agreed, and nodded, and he stepped back and hit the little fellow a good blow on the head. I threw away the flowers and we dragged him into the wood. He had ten shillings on him and we took half each. He looked very bad, so the other fellow said: 'We had better put him away,' and I said: 'Yes, he may be in awful pain, such a white-faced fellow as he is.' So we knocked the life out of him, and the other fellow went off Marlborough way and I went into Swindon and had such a dinner as I hadn't had for weeks, rabbit and new potatoes and a bit of curry. . . . Did you ever hear about that?

"Get on my mind? Why, I never meant the fellow any harm and I filled my belly.

"Can you tell me where there is a lone road where

I can make a bit of fire? I don't like the dust and noise of these motor cars." . . .

Away he went, halting a little, and yet, from behind, having an absurd resemblance to a child, which his cheerfulness reinforced.

Later in the evening I found him just awakened from his first sleep, near a dead fire that had been no bigger than a pigeon's nest.

"What a country this is," he said indignantly, but with good humour.

"There are not enough sticks in this wood to warm the only man that wants them. I suppose they use all the firing to keep the pheasants warm. Hark at them! If I was a rich man I wouldn't keep such birds . . .

"England is not such a place as it was when I was a young man. It is not half the size for one thing. Why, when I was a young man, you could go up a lane with a long dog or two and pick up a bit of supper and firing and nothing said. The country seemed to belong to me in those days, but now I might as well be in Africa. I am worse off than the labourers now, except that I have got more sense than they have, singing their silly old songs, like this." Then he sang with perhaps mock sentimentality a frail little peasant song, full of the smallness of lonely, small lives:

> Mary come into the field
> To work along of I,
> Digging up mangold wurzels,
> For they be a-growing high.
>> Dig 'em up by the roots,
>> Dig 'em up by the roots,
>> Put in your spade,
>> Don't be afraid,
>> Dig 'em up by the roots.

Our master is a hard one,
He pays us very small;
And if we stop a moment
We hear his voice to call —
    "Dig 'em up by the roots," etc.

We work all day together,
Till all the light is past;
And only going homewards
Do we join hands at last.
    "Dig 'em up by the roots," etc.

For many years we 've been sweethearts
And worked the fields along,
And sometimes even now
Mary will sing the old song —
    "Dig 'em up by the roots," etc.

"What is that to the song about 'the swift and
silly doe' my old father used to sing to us, or about
'Gentle Jenny,' the mare that threw the fellow that
wasn't going to pay for her hire. No, there is no
room in England now for toe-rags like me and you;
if you wanted to, you couldn't sleep on Bearsted
Green to-night."

Later in the year, on August Bank Holiday, I found
him at an inn, where a farm bailiff was treating the
labourers to much ale. The landlord had a young
relative down from London, who sang a song in the
bar about a skylark who was to take a message to his
mother in heaven. At this the tramp melted a little:
the pale face of the singer and the high shrill voice
made an entrance somewhere, and he tried to join in
the song. But towards evening he was to be found
sticking pins through his cheek and ears and into his
arms, and offering, for a small sum, to stick them into
any part whatsoever; or, lying on his back and

twisting his head back—the muscles in his throat croaking all the time like frogs—to pick up with his teeth a penny that lay on the floor. The bailiff had caught him. He did odd jobs about the farm, and lived in a forgotten cottage, too far away from anywhere to keep pigs in. But he slept in the cottage only on one or two nights in the seven. During the rest of the week he was to be found at night under the edge of a copse, beside a little fire, reminding himself of the old, roomy England which he used to know.

CHAPTER VI

ALL day the winter seemed to have gone. The horses' hoofs on the moist, firm road made a clear "cuck-oo" as they rose and fell; and far off, for the first time in the year, a ploughboy, who remembered spring and knew that it would come again, shouted "Cuckoo! cuckoo!"

A warm wind swept over the humid pastures and red sand-pits on the hills and they gleamed in a lightly muffled sun. Once more in the valleys the ruddy farmhouses and farm-buildings seemed new and fair again, and the oast-house cones stood up as prophets of spring, since the south wind had turned all their white vanes towards the north, and they felt the sea that lay—an easy journey on such a day— beyond the third or fourth wooded ridge in the south. The leaves of goose-grass, mustard, vetch, dog's mercury, were high above the dead leaves on hedge banks. Primrose and periwinkle were blossoming. Like flowers were the low ash-tree boles where the axe had but lately cut off the tall rods; flower-like and sweet also the scent from the pits where labourers dipped the freshly peeled ash poles in tar. In the elms, sitting crosswise on a bough, sang thrush and missel thrush; in the young corn, the larks; the robins in the thorns; and in all the meadows the guttural notes of the rooks were mellowed by love and the sun.

Making deep brown ruts across the empty green fields came the long wagons piled high with faggots; the wheels rumbled; the harness jingled and shone; the horses panted and the carters cracked their whips.

Soon would the first chiff-chaff sing in the young larches; at evening the calm, white, majestic young clouds should lie along the horizon in a clear and holy air; and climbing a steep hill at that hour, the walker should see a window, as it were, thrown open in the sky and hear a music that should silence thought and even regret—as when, on the stage, a window is opened and someone invisible is heard to sing a heavy-laden song below it.

But as I walked and the wind fell for the sunset, the path led me under high, stony beeches. The air was cool and still and moist and waterish dark, and no bird sang. A wood-pigeon spread out his barry tail as he ascended perpendicularly to a hidden place among the branches, and then there was no sound. The waterish half-light seemed to have lasted for ever and to have an eternity ahead. Through the trees a grassy, deeply-rutted road wound downwards, and at the edge the ruts were broad and full of dark water. Still retaining some corruption of the light of the sky upon its surface, that shadowed water gave an immense melancholy to the wood. The reflections of the beeches across it were as the bars of a cage that imprisoned some child of light. It was but a few inches deep of rain, and yet, had it been a legendary pool, or had a drowned woman's hair been stamped into the mud at its edge and left a green forehead exposed, it could not have stained and filled the air more tragically. The cold, the silence, the leaflessness found an expression in that clouded shining surface among the ruts. Life and death seemed to contend there, and I recalled a dream which I had lately dreamed.

I dreamed that someone had cut the cables that anchored me to such tranquillity as had been mine, and that I was drifted out upon an immensity of desolation and solitude. I was without hope, without even the energy of despair that might in time have given birth to hope. But in that desolation I found one business: to search for a poison that should kill slowly, painlessly, and unexpectedly. In that search I lost sight of what had persuaded me to it; yet when at last I succeeded, I took a draught and went out into the road and began to walk. A calm fell upon me such as I had sometimes found in June thunderstorms on lonely hills, or in midnights when I stepped for a moment after long foolish labours to my door, and heard the nightingales singing out from the Pleiades that overhung the wood, and saw the flower-faced owl sitting on the gate. I walked on, not hastening with a too great desire nor lingering with a too careful quietude. It was as yet early morning, and the wheat sheaves stood on the gentle hills like yellow-haired women kneeling to the sun that was about to rise. Now and then I passed the corners of villages, and sometimes at windows and through doorways I saw the faces of men and women I had known and seemed to forget, and they smiled and were glad, but not more glad than I. Labouring in the fields also were men whose faces I was happy to recognize and see smiling with recognition. And very sweet it was to go on thus, at ease, knowing neither trouble nor fatigue. I could have gone on, it seemed, for ever, and I wished to live so for ever, when suddenly I remembered the poison. Then of each one I met I begged a remedy. Some reminded me that formerly I had made a poor thing of life, and said that it was too late. Others supposed that I jested. A few asked me to stay with them and rest. The sky and the earth, and the men and women drank of the poison that I had drunken, so that I could not endure the use of my eyes, and I entered a shop to buy some desperate remedy that should end all at once, when, seeing behind the counter a long-dead friend in wedding attire, I awoke.

Even so in the long wet ruts did the false hope of spring contend with the shadows: even so at last did it end, when the dead leaves upon the trees began to stir madly in the night wind, with the sudden, ghastly motion of burnt paper on a still fire when a draught stirs it in a silent room at night; and even the nearest trees seemed to be but fantastic hollows in the misty air.

CHAPTER VII

OUT of the midst of pale wheat lands and tussocky
meadow, intersected by streams which butter-bur and
marigold announce, and soared over by pewit and
lark and the first swallows with their delicate laughter,
rises the grim, decorated church, of the same colour
as the oak trees round about. White and grey headstones, some of great age, bow to it in the churchyard,
and seem mutely to crave for the shelter from the
north-east wind. There is much room within. All
the headstones and those whom they commemorate
might find places and not crowd out the little congregation. In one transept a knight and lady are
taking their ease in stone, and looking up at the
gaudy arms above them. They came early to the
church. From the memorial inscriptions on pavement
and walls, it would seem that the church belongs to a
later great family, still living near. Soldiers, sailors,
landowners, clergymen even, they take possession at
their death; from 1623 they have flocked here, and
the names of their virtues live after them; tyrants
perhaps in their lifetime, they have the air of being
idols now, and they outnumber the prophets on the
window glass. The service proceeds in the accustomed
decent manner, with nasal lesson and humming prayer.
Then comes the hymn:

> Through all the changing scenes of life—

One woman's ambitious, shrill treble voice that seems
ever about to fall and yet continues to maintain its airy

43

height, leads the congregation to unusual adventures of song. The church is dense with emotion; ordinary gentlemen, shopkeepers, labourers and their wives, men and women of all degrees of endurance, chivalry, good intention, uncertain aims, sentimental virtuousness, hypocrisy not dissevered from hardship, vanity not ignorant of tenderness, hard ambition, the desire to be respected—men and women throw all kinds of strange meaning, heartfelt and present, imaginative, retrospective, expectant, into the vague words of the hymn. I can see one strong man shouting it with an expression as if he were pole-axing a bull. His neighbour, a frail, tearful woman, sings as if it absolves her from the tears with which she marred not only her own life. One aged woman made it clearly an expression of the nothingness of mankind, a ridicule and blasphemy of life, as if she had repeated the words of the old play:

> Where is now Solomon, in wisdom so excellent?
> Where is now Samson, in battle so strong?
> Where is now Absalom, in beauty resplendent?
> Where is now good Jonathan, hid so long?
> Where is now Cæsar, in victory triumphing?
> Where is now Dives, in dishes so dainty?
> Where is now Tully, in eloquence exceeding?
> Where is now Aristotle, learned so deeply?
> What emperors, kings, and dukes in times past,
> What earls and lords, and captains of war,
> What popes and bishops, all at the last
> In the twinkling of an eye are fled so far?
> How short a feast is this worldly joying?
> Even as a shadow it passeth away,
> Depriving a man of gifts everlasting,
> Leading to darkness and not to day!
> O meat of worms, O heap of dust,
> O like to dew, climb not too high.

Other faces express complacency, hope, the newness of a solution of this thing life, grim, satisfied despair, even a kind of vanity. All these men and women might agree at a political meeting; here they differ each from the rest, and every one of the gods in all the mythologies must be gladdened or angered at some part of the hymn by the meaning of this or that worshipper; Odin, Apollo, Diana, Astarte, the Cat, the Beetle, and the rest revive, in whatever Tartarus they are thrust, at these strange sounds.

The last of the congregation left, but I could still hear the hymn wandering feebly among the tall arches and up and about, apparently restless, as if it sought to get out and away, but in vain. The high grey stone and those delicate windows made a cage; and the human voices were as those of Seifelmolouk and his memlooks, when the giant king kept them in cages because the sound of their lamentation seemed to him the most melodious music, and he thought them birds. Inexorably, the fancy held me that some gaunt giant, fifty cubits high, kept men and women in this cage because he loved to hear their voices expressing moods he knew nothing of. Not more caged are the five brown bells in the tower, with mute, patient heads like cows, their names being Solitude, Tranquillity, Duty, Harmony, Joy.

CHAPTER VIII

GARLAND DAY

THE sun had not risen though it had long been proclaimed, when the old road led us into a moist wood that grew on the hillside, and here and there overhung a perpendicular chalk cliff. The soil was black and crisp with old beech mast, and out of it grew the clear, grave, green leaves of anemone and dog's mercury and spurge and hyacinth and primroses, in places so dense that the dim earth below them seemed to be some deep lake's water. All the anemones were bowed and rosy. The blue bells were plated with rain. The dark spurge leaves were crowned by pale green flowers. The primroses grew, twenty in a cluster, on long flushed stalks; each petal was perfect, and down their leaves the raindrops slid and glittered or gleamed duskily. Arching above these, the low brier branches carried sharp green young foliage. A shadowed pool in one of the hollows was hardly to be distinguished from the dark earth, except that it was covered with white crowfoot flowers as with five minutes' snow.

From among the flowers ascended straight stony rods of ash, their ancient stoles bossy and hollowed like skulls, and covered with moss; and from the purple encrusted ash flowers wood-pigeons shook the rain down to the leaves beneath. Amongst the ash trees were hazels, new leaved, their olive stems gloomily shining.

46

Over all, the ancient beeches stood up with hard sculptured boles supporting story after story of branch and shade which were traversed at the top and at the fringes by fair fresh leaves. The rain had run down the main trunks for generations, and made paths of green and black that tried to gleam. Here and there, low down, the beeches extended long priestly branches clothed in leaf, still and curved, to call for silence in the cool, shadowy, crystal air.

Far away among the branches whitened the chalk cliffs. On this side and on that, immense mossy boulders made tables for thrushes and cast perfect shadows.

High up in the beeches, the invisible wood wrens sang, and their songs were as if, overhead in the stainless air, little waves of pearls dropped and scattered and shivered on a shore of pearls. Below them the wood-pigeons began to coo—with notes that were but as rounded bubbles emerging from the silence and lost again. Just within hearing, in the hawthorn hedge of the wood, blackbirds were singing: they opened with the most high, arrogating notes that slowly rolled on to noble ends, when suddenly they laughed and ceased; again and again they began so, and again and again they laughed, as if they had grown too wise to believe utterly in noble things. As we went deeper into the wood they ceased, and those moist shades welcomed us as if they held what we desired.

The trees were very old; their leaves were fresh and wet as when beauty and joy shed a few tears. The soil was centuries deep in black beech mast; the herbage seemed to have been born from it in that

very hour. The boulders had stood among the primroses so long that the thrushes had chiselled shallow
cups in them as they fed there in the mornings;
they were embossed with the most tender green and
golden moss. The shadows were as solemn and im-
perturbable as to a child a cathedral, when he first
steps into its solitude alone, and a god is created anew
out of his marvelling; and yet the hems of their
mantles, where they swept the ground, disclosed a
flashing underside of crystals newly born. And for
ourselves—we seemed to be home from a long exile,
and the pains of it, such as they were, turned like
the shadows into crystal. Here, then, was the land
to which had fled those children who once bore our
names, who were our companions in the days when
sunshine was more than wine had ever been since,
and they left us long ago, not suddenly, but so
strangely, that we knew not that they were far off:
hither those children had fled, and their companions
of that time; here they had been hiding these many
years; abiding here they had become immortal in the
green-fledged antique wood, and we had come back
to them. Perhaps they recognized us: perhaps they
re-entered these bodies of ours. For once more the
cuckoo was clear, golden, joyous. When we heard the
blackbird again we did not quarrel with the laugh at
his own solemnity, since it was not there. It was not
memory, nor hope. Memory perished, and hope that
never rests lay asleep; and winds blew softly from over
Lethe and breathed upon our eyelids, coming as
delicate intercessors between us and life. We forgot
that ours had been the sin of Alcyone and Ceyx who,
in their proud happiness, called one another *Zeus!*
and *Here!* and for that were cast down by the gods.

Once again we did so, for this was the wood of youth, and in the old streets of the soul where the grass grows among the long-untrqdden stones, and in the doorways of deserted homes, the sound of footsteps and the click of a frequented latch was heard.

And yonder is the wide prospect again, and the dawn—the green hedges starred with white stitchwort flower, misty with the first hawthorn clusters, a-flutter with whitethroat, wild with the warbling of the black-cap in their depths; wide, lustrous meadows dimmed by cuckoo-flowers, and at the edges of them the oaks beginning to bud and their branches like great black brands about to break into golden flame; and about the oaks that stood in the midst of them the grass waving in the sun like brooks plunging from their roots; farmhouses known only by their encircling apple trees all in bloom; radiant pools where the sand-piper laughed; woods where the oak and ash waded deep in the translucent green of the undergrowth's rising tide and even then glowed with brown and unborn greens, and the nightingale sang far with-drawn, and at the edge the hurdlemaker worked by his thatched cote; and ridge beyond ridge of hills cloudily wooded; and over all the low sky like a blue bowl just emptied of its cream.

And as we sat at breakfast the village children came up the path between borders dense with tall yellow leopard's bane and red honesty and sang by the windows:

> Please to remember the first of May,
> For the first of May is Garland Day.

And they carried garlands of ivy entwined among

bluebells and cowslips from the moist warm copses
and the meadows.

On the twin vanes of the oasts, one pointing east,
one north, the south wind and the west wind were
asleep in one another's arms.

CHAPTER IX

THE chestnut blossom is raining steadily and noise-lessly down upon a path whose naked pebbles receive mosaic of emerald light from the interlacing boughs. At intervals, once or twice an hour, the wings of a lonely swallow pass that way, when alone the shower stirs from its perpendicular fall. Cool and moist, the perfumed air flows, without lifting the most nervous leaf or letting fall a suspended bead of the night's rain from a honeysuckle bud. In an indefinite sky of grey, through which one ponderous cloud billows into sight and is lost again, no sun shines: yet there is light—I know not whence; for the brass trappings of the horses beam so as to be extinguished in their own fire. There is no song in wood or sky. Some one of summer's wandering voices—bullfinch or willow wren—might be singing, but unheard, at least un-realized. From the dead-nettle spires, with dull green leaves stained by purple and becoming more and more purple towards the crest, which is of a sombre uniform purple, to the elms reposing at the horizon, all things have bowed the head, hushed, settled into a perfect sleep. Those elms are just visible, no more. The path has no sooner emerged from one shade than another succeeds, and so, on and on, the eye wins no broad dominion.

It is a land that uses a soft compulsion upon the passer-by, a compulsion to meditation, which is necessary before he is attached to a scene rather featureless, to a land that hence owes much of its power to a mood of generous reverie which it bestows. And yet it is a land that gives much. Companionable it is, reassuring to the solitary; he soon has a feeling of ease and seclusion there. The cool-leaved wood! The limitless, unoccupied fields of marsh marigold, seen through the trees, most beautiful when the evening rain falls slowly, dimming and almost putting out the lustrous bloom! Gold of the minute willows underfoot! Leagues of lonely grass where the slow herds tread the daisies and spare them yet!

Towards night, under the sweet rain, at this warm, skyless close of the day, the trees, far off in an indolent, rolling landscape, stand as if disengaged from the world, in a reticent and pensive repose.

But suddenly the rain has ceased. In an old, dense wood the last horizontal beams of the sun embrace the trunks of the trees and they glow red under their moist ceiling of green. A stile to be crossed at its edge, where a little stream, unseen, sways the stiff exuberant angelica that grows from it, gives the word to pause, and with a rush the silence and the solitude fill the brain. The wood is of uncounted age; the ground on which it stands is more ancient than the surrounding fields, for it rises and falls stormily, with huge boulders here and there; not a path intrudes upon it; the undergrowth is impenetrable to all but fox and bird and this cool red light about the trunks of the trees. Far away a gate is loudly shut, and the rich blue evening comes on and severs me irrevocably from all but the light in the old wood and the ghostly white cow-parsley flowers suspended on unseen stalks. And there, among the trees and their shadows, not understood, speaking a forgotten tongue, old dreads and formless awes and fascinations discover themselves and address the comfortable soul, troubling it, recalling to it unremembered years not so long past but that in the end it settles down into a gloomy tranquillity and satisfied discontent, as when we see the place where we were unhappy as children once. Druid and devilish deity and lean wild beast, harmless now, are revolving many memories with me under the strange, sudden red light in the old wood, and not more remote is the league-deep emerald sea-cave from the storm above than I am from the world.

CHAPTER X

IN A FARMYARD

WE waited to let the forty cows go past, each of them pausing to lick the forehead of the strawberry cow that leaned over the gate of her stall and lowed continually concerning her newly-born white calf. But so slow they were in their wanton, obedient movement to the milking-shed that we turned and found another path, and thus surprised a pond lying deep among tansy flowers, grey nettles, and billows of conquering bramble and brier.

The farmyard was always dusty, or deep with ridgy mire, from the trampling of men and horses and cows in the streets that wound among its cart-lodges, stables, stalls, milking-sheds, and barns all glowing with mature tiles, and ricks gleaming with amber thatch. But in a corner lay unused, older than them all, the long-headed and snaky-bodied pond. We learned to know that pond.

Sometimes, when summer has honoured the water with a perfect suit of emerald green, that pond shows itself to be a monstrous, coiled, primeval thing, lying undisturbed, and content to be still and contemplative. Often has the monster been driven away—by draining; often has it returned, still a green, coiled, primeval being that disappears suddenly in November and leaves a soft, dark pool. Some have ventured to intrude upon the monster, to fish for the sleepy carp which are found when it has been driven from its nest of purple mud; but they fish in vain.

The solitary, dying ash tree at the edge of the pond seems, by day, when the monster is powerful there in the summer, to be but the skeleton of an old victim; or, in the winter, the sad and twisted nymph of the water. But every night, like any dreaming child or musing lover, though not perhaps so happily, is it let into a varied, strange, exalted paradise.

You may see it—on still evenings when the mist prevails over all things except the robin's song, and makes even that more melancholy—or when the songs of many nightingales besiege, enter, and possess the house and the deserted farmyard—or when the cold and entirely silent air under a purple November sky chills the blood, so that friendship and hope and purposes are all in vain as in an opiate dream—then you may see the ash tree take heart. It has the air of one going home upon a lonely road that will not end in loneliness. Those bare and stiff, decaying branches are digits pointing homeward through the sky; the tree forgets the monster at its feet and the children who laugh and the supremacy of the buildings round about. It might seem, with those extended branches, to be a self-torturing and aspiring fanatic who had endured thus for uncounted days and nights, and has his vision at last. For, when night is perfect, the tree exults, and though it is perhaps not joyous, it is as one of those great sorrowful temperaments— of soldier, or explorer, or humorist—so active and inexorable that they may claim kinship with the truly joyous ones. If it is still sad, it is "endiademed with woe." How large and satanic it is beside the heavy rounded oaks and the stately, feminine elms and the lovely limes.

Even so might a philosopher heighten and lord it,

travelling in Charon's ship along with deflated tyrants and rhetoricians and bold and crimson animals born to eat provinces and to poison worms; even so, Ossian and Arthur and Cuchullain and Achilles triumph over men that were yesterday on thrones and chariots. Often have I seen the tree, and it alone, giving character to the whole valley and filling the land as a bell fills a cathedral or as the droning of a bee fills a lily.

> With him enthroned
> Sat sable-vested night, eldest of things,
> The consort of his reign.

My little thoughts seem to be drawn up among the black branches like twittering birds going to rest in some high cliff that is a chief pillar of the fabric of the night. Half dead and threatened though it be, surely the spirit of it, which is to many a broad and tragical night as the arm of a great painter to his picture, will survive not only me and my words but the tree itself. I have approached it on some moonlit midnights, when the sky was so deep that the tall oaks were as weeds at the bottom of an unfathomed sea, and it has stood up erect and puissant, as if it were the dreamer at one with all he sees, in a world of blind men with open eyes. Then, as the autumn dawn arrived it was still looking towards Orion; defrauded, indeed, for a time of its vision, but not of its glory. The swaying cows wandered to the milking-sheds. The little bats ran to and fro in the air and made their little snipping and drumming sounds. It was light; but the ash tree was not utterly cast down; it still walked in the way of the stars; it was inscribed in solemn characters upon the sun that rose up red in the mist.

CHAPTER XI

THIS is one of the tracts of country which are discovered by few except such as study the railway maps of England in order to know what to avoid. On those maps it is one of several large triangular sections which railways bound, but have not entered. All day long the engines scream along their boundaries, and at night wave fiery arms to the sky, as if to defend a forbidden place or a sanctuary. Within there is peace, and a long ancient lane explores it, with many windings and turnings back, as if it were a humble, diffident inquirer, fortunately creeping on, aiming at some kind of truth and not success, yet without knowing what truth is when he starts. Here it hesitates by a little pool, haunted, as is clear from the scribbled footprints on the shore, only by moorhen and wagtail, and, in the spindle trees beside it, by a witty thrush; there it goes joyously forward, straight among lines of tall oaks and compact thorns; then it turns to climb a hill from which all the country it has passed is visible first, meadow and withy copse and stream, and next the country which it has yet to pass—a simple dairy land with green grass, green woods, and stout grey haystacks round the pale farms. But in a little while it winds, confused again under high maple and dogwood hedges, downhill, as if it had already forgotten what the hilltop showed. On the level again the hollow wood which the willow

wren fills with his little lonely song has to be pene-
trated; the farmyard must be passed through, and the
spirit of the road looks in at the dairy window and
sees the white disks of cream in the pans and the cool-
armed maid lifting a cheese; and yet another farmyard
it loiters in, watching the roses and plume-poppy and
lupin of the front garden, going between the stables
and the barn, and there spreading out as if it had
resolved to cease and always watch the idle wagon,
the fair-curved hay-rakes leaning against the wall, and
the fowls which are the embodiment of senseless
reverie—when lo! the path goes straight across wide
and level pastures, with a stream at its side. Seen
afar off, losing itself among the elms that watch over
the hillside church, the little white road is as some
quiet, hermit saint, just returned from long seclusion,
and about to take up his home for ever and ever in
the chancel; but when we reach the place, he is still
as far away, still uncertain in the midst of the corn
below. At the charlock-yellow summit the road seems
to lead into the sky, where the white ladders are let
down from the sun.

The ways of such a road—when the June grass is
high and in the sun it is invisible except for its
blueness and its buttercups, and the chaffinch, the
corn-bunting, and yellowhammer, the sleepiest-voiced
birds, are most persistent—easily persuade the mind
that it alone is travelling, travelling through an ideal
country, belonging to itself and beyond the power of
the world to destroy. The few people whom we see,
the mower, the man hoeing his onion-bed in a spare
half-hour at midday, the children playing "Jar-jar-
winkle" against a wall, the women hanging out
clothes—these the very loneliness of the road has

prepared us for turning into creatures of dream; it costs an effort to pass the time of day with them, and they being equally unused to strange faces are not loquacious, and so the moment they are passed they are no more real than the men and women of pastoral:

> He leads his Wench a Country Horn-pipe Round,
> About a May-pole on a Holy-day;
> Kissing his lovely Lasse (with Garlands Crownd)
> With whooping heigh-ho singing Care away;
> Thus doth he passe the merry month of May:
>   And all th' yere after in delight and joy,
>   (Scorning a King) he cares for no annoy.

The most credible inhabitants are Mertilla, Florimel, Corin, Amaryllis, Dorilus, Doron, Daphnis, Silvia, and Aminta, and shepherds singing to their flocks

> Lays of sweet love and youth's delightful heat.

Yonder the road curves languidly between hedges and broad fringes of green, and along it an old man guides the cattle in to afternoon milking. They linger to crop the wayside grass and he waits, but suddenly resumes his walk and they obey, now hastening with tight udders and looking from side to side. They turn under the archway of a ruined abbey, and low as if they enjoy the reverberation, and disappear. I never see them again; but the ease, the remoteness, the colour of the red cattle in the green road, the slowness of the old cowman, the timelessness of that gradual movement under the fourteenth-century arch, never vanish.

Of such things the day is made, not of milestones and antiquities. Isolated, rapt from the earth, perhaps, by the very fatigue which at the end restores us to it forcibly, the mind goes on seeing and remembering these things.

Here the cattle stand at the edge of a pond and the tench swim slowly above the weeds amongst them as they stand. The sun strikes down upon the glassy water, but cannot take away the coolness of the reeds about the margin. Under the one oak in the meadow above, the farmer sits with his dog, so still that the dabchick does not dive and the water vole nibbles' the reed, making a small sound, the only one.

There five little girls play the lovers' game on a green in front of their cottages. One of them kneels down and cries quietly; the others hold hands and circle round her, singing:

Poor Mary sits a-weeping, a-weeping, a-weeping,
Poor Mary sits a-weeping, by the bright shining shore.

Oh tell us what you 're weeping for, weeping for, weeping for,
Oh tell us what you 're weeping for, by the bright shining shore.

Then the little "poor Mary," with her face still in her apron, takes up the singing, the others still moving round her:

I 'm weeping for my true love, my true love, my true love,
I 'm weeping for my true love, by the bright shining shore.

Then the others sing to her:

Get up and choose a better one, a better one, a better one,
Get up and choose a better one, by the bright shining shore.

At this, Mary rises, and chooses one of those from the ring, and the two stand in the middle, holding each others' hands crossed, while the others sing:

Your true love is a shepherd's cross, a shepherd's cross a shepherd's
    cross,
Your true love is a shepherd's cross, by the bright shining shore.

So Mary now takes her place in the ring; her true love becomes "poor Mary," and chooses another lover amidst the same song; and at last, when all have been Marys and true lovers, with resolute faces, they scatter carelessly and forget. Finding some marbles in a roadside crevice, I ask one child to play, but she says that marbles are not played after Good Friday. A white cow rests beside, so much in love with peace that it grazes lying down. On the other side of the road the bacon hisses and smells from a farmhouse whose mountainous thatch makes a cool cave of tranquillity; on the sunny slope the starlings who have honeycombed the thatch, whistle or creep in with food or straw. Not one path disturbs the unfrequented verdure of the green, though the road winds lazily round it.

Yonder, up a steep field, goes a boy birdnesting in a double hedge, stooping to the nettles for the white-throat's eggs, straining high among the hawthorns for a dove's. He does not hasten. Now and then he calls "cuckoo," not a timorous note, but lusty like the bird's own: and now he lies down to suck a thrush's egg. He will not take the robin's eggs, "or I shall get my arm broken," he says. A cruel game, but so long as he loves it with all his heart perhaps it is forgiven him, and in a few years he will never again go slowly up that field, forgetful of schoolmaster, father and mother, and the greatness of man.

At noon there is a hamlet in front. On one side of it the church thrusts a golden weathercock high into the blue sky, and with his proud and jolly head up-lifted towards the north the bird flames and exults; on the other side, tall beeches give out the sleepy noise of rooks. Straight ahead "The White Hart," a

white inn with heavy, overhanging thatch, divides the
road in two. Those white walls can never cease to
glow; they have persuaded the sun to sleep under
those eaves for ever like the carter on the bench.
The sign-board hangs silent, but the sign has melted
away. A wagon stands by the door; the wagoner
holds a chestnut mare with one hand, with the other
he slowly tilts the glittering tankard and shows all
of his brown throat throbbing; the hostess watches.

The low white kitchen is cut in two by a tall, semi-
circular settle, to which the hostess returns and with a
round elm table between her and the fire she lops
fine greens into a pail. A tenanted fireplace is better
than a cold one on any day of the year, and it is cool
in the window seat between the ale and the wind.
Outside lies the little road, waiting for me. And
now we go on together, the road having still the
advantage of me, though it has poured no libation.

All through the long afternoon that land offers
symbols of peace, security, and everlastingness. Tall
hedges half hidden in a rising tide of long, starry
herbage, ponds where the probing carp make the lily
leaves rise and flap, wide meadows where the cows
wander half a mile an hour, vast green cumulus clouds
with round summits here and there disclosing infinite
receding glooms of blue — these with their continual
presence store the mind, giving it not only that
poignant joy in which half consciously we know that
never again shall we be just here and thus, but the
joy, too, of knowing that we take these things along
with us to the end —

> Then whate'er
> Poor laws divide the public year,
> Whose revolutions wait upon

The wild turns of the wanton sun;
There all the year is love's long spring,
There all the year love's nightingales shall sit and sing.

On that poem of Crashaw's to his ivory-handed mistress runs my thought as the road, towards evening, once more progresses without any hedges between it and the fields, when a broad double hedge or narrow copse of oak and ash departs at a right angle from the way. Up to the briers and thorns at the hem of the trees comes the close, cool yellow grass and obtains a shadow there. Out on to that grass the blackbirds have strayed and are straying farther and farther; the rabbits, too, are well away from shelter, hopping a few steps and crouching. In the hedge itself a hedge-sparrow just once lets loose its frail dewy song, a nightingale utters one phrase of marvelling and is still. The musky wild roses star all the hedge and the scent begins to wander in the moist air with the scent of honeysuckle and of shadowy grasses. Under a now misted sky that makes the light seem to dwell no longer in it but in the grass, the flat, yellow field running to the little wood is a place impregnable and inaccessible. Invisible walls shut me off, though no hedge intervenes; no dreadful barrier could do it more effectually. It would be as easy to step into the past as into this candid field, a withdrawn world with its own sun.

A mile farther a little town stands upon the edge of this enclosed land. A brook runs down to its edge and half encircles it. Clean and fair, shining with linen, the meadows come right up to the town which turns its back upon them, with long rows of beans and peas dividing the yellow houses from one another. The chimney smoke rises above the criss-cross roofs of stone and thatch and then travels round the church tower, which emerges from the houses like some grave schoolmaster out of his children, most of them thronging close and others wandering, in wedge or line, into the fields. In the town the road loses itself, bewildered among islands made by inns and groups of cottages, the church and the shops. Among these pour a flock of sheep, swelling as the streets enlarge, contracting as they contract, and always filling them. Within the town there is not a blade of grass, nor a garden, nor a tree; and yet the richly burning roofs, the grey or white walls, the sign of "The Spotted Cow," or the sign of "The Sun," make not an interruption but a diversion in the fields, when suddenly, between two white walls, shines the green evening land, and across it a busy train rushes and vanishes with long, delicious, dying reverberations among the dark woods and rosy clouds at the horizon.

CHAPTER XII

THE sun rose two hours ago, but he is not to be found in the sky. Rather he seems to have disembodied himself and to be lazily concealed in the sweet mist that lies white and luminous over the half-mile of level meadows at the foot of this hill. Those meadows are brown with yet untouched grasses, grey and silken with the placid ruffled waves of yesterday's new swaths, and liquid emerald where the hay has already been carted; and now the brown, now the grey, now the emerald warms and becomes visible under the feet of the light that dwells in the mist. Beyond the level rises a low but sudden hill of large, round-topped, colourless, misty trees, known by their outline alone, and in the heart of them a moving gleam as of sudden surf now and then, for there also the sun is wandering and hiding himself but not his light. I turn my head and, looking again, the sun is once more in the sky, the mist has gone. The vast, hunched, hot, purring summer country is clearly enjoying the light and warmth. The swallows flying are joyous and vivid in colour and form as if I had the eyes of some light-hearted painter of the world's dawn. Where the gleam was, that haunt of the sun's, that half-hour's inn to which he turns from the long white road of the sky to rest, is seen to be the white farmhouse that stands in the midst of woods and ricks.

Yet, though so clear, the house, half a mile off, seems to have been restored by this fair and early light and the cooing of doves to the seeming happy age in which it was built. The long, tearing crow of the cock, the clink of dairy pans, the palpitating, groaning shout of the shepherd, *Ho! ho! ho! ho! ho!* now and then, even the whirr of the mowing machines, sound as if the distance that sweetens them were the distance of time and not only of space. They set a tune on this fair morning to "What a dainty life the milkmaid leads" or that old song:

> Pack clouds away, and welcome day!
> With night we banish sorrow.
> Sweet air, blow soft; mount, lark, aloft
> To give my love good morrow.
> Wings from the wind to please her mind,
> Notes from the lark I 'll borrow:
> Bird, prune thy wing, nightingale, sing,
> To give my love good morrow.
> To give my love good morrow,
> Notes from them all I 'll borrow.
>
> Wake from thy nest, robin redbreast!
> Sing, birds, in every furrow,
> And from each bill let music shrill
> Give my fair love good morrow.
> Blackbird and thrush in every bush,
> Stare, linnet, and cock-sparrow,
> You pretty elves, amongst yourselves
> Sing my fair love good morrow.
> To give my love good morrow,
> Sing, birds, in every furrow.

In those days, when the house was built, the poets were mainly townsmen, preferring the town. Of the modern sad passion of Nature they had nothing: they loved the fields in their season. They went out into the country and in their *fêtes-champêtres* here was something gay and foreign from us, the thought of which calls up a vision of fields more unspoiled than they are now. There were elves in those days; country people saw them, if poets failed. If you were returning home after nightfall from a day's shooting, you might see the torches among the oaks that lit the king of the cats to his grave. The country had always been there and was to be there for ever. Men greeted it and smiled as once they greeted Helen, not thinking of her immortality. And there—yonder, half a mile away—lingers that age. I see it in the green and silver wheat, and its glimmering, rustling hurry, and in the bright path beside; the very noises of a gun rolling and breaking up and embedding themselves in the dense wood cannot mutilate it, but rather hint that somewhere, where the echoes last play, a spirit of mirth is in hiding still.

The farmer himself confirms the superstition. Though nearly seventy, he is staunch and straight, and spending most of his day on horseback, with his calm, large-featured, sandstone face, filling easily and handsomely with clear-souled anger and delight, he suggests the thought of a Centaur, an impossible, noble dream of horse and man created by a god dissatisfied with man and beast. Thirty centuries ago such a man, so marvellously in harmony with the earth, would have gone down in men's memories as a demi-god or the best-loved of the fauns. His voice rings over the meadows or across the table at the inn as strong as a cow's, as deep and humming and sweet as a bee's in a chimney. When he passes by men look at him, I think, as if he cast no shadow, so compact of light is he. He has known sorrow, he has known pains that threaten to crack the brain, but never melancholy. There is a kinct of gaiety in his sorrow even as in his joy; for sorrow changes him only as a shadow changes a merry brook. He breathes of a day when men had not so far outstripped the lark and nightingale in heaviness as we have done. His jesting bathes the room or the lane in the light of a Golden Age and the freshness of all the May days we can never recover. Nor do I know anything human more pleasant than his grave smiling as he stands in the newly reaped cornfields under the last light and sees the large purple land and takes it all unto himself, and then turns without a sigh and, drawing a long draught of his own cider in the cool granary, drinks deep. He rises early and yet is as cheerful when he goes first afield as when he goes to bed.

His house, dark with panelling and heavy furniture of every generation since it was built, would be gloomy were it not for his blithe sentiment about the past. He speaks of the long-dead generations not as if they were names, but so that they are known certainly to have lived and worked and enjoyed. That one planted the spreading oak, that globed green world of nightingale and willow wren and dove; that added the knolled pasture and cut the deep, stony lane that leads to it through the brook; another built the fruit wall and bought the copy of *Tristram Shandy* that stands with a hundred other books in the dining-room. The books themselves are good to look at, all of them original or early editions. There is *The Whole Duty of Man* and many sermons, Prior, *The Spectator*, Thomson's *Seasons*, Fielding, *The Rambler*, *The Task*, *The Deserted Village*, *The Waverley Novels*, Dickens, and nothing later than *In Memoriam*; at that the family seems to have stopped buying books. He knows them shrewdly enough, but it is as what the family has approved and lived on that he values them. Never was a man who seemed to take his mortality so happily and naturaly. One day, showing me a small hoard of ancient things, he brought out a tray of coins, none earlier than Charles II, but each connected with one or another of the family. Amongst them was a modern sixpence. That was his third deposit, after the guinea and the groat, and he was too much pleased with these slender memorials not to do his own part in continuing them. "What," he said carelessly, "would they think of me in a hundred years' time if I had not put a sixpence in?" And he smiled lightly as if he had been on a hill and seen the long tracts of time ahead and his farm and strangers of his own blood working in its fields.

CHAPTER XIII

POPPIES

THE earliest mower had not risen yet; the only sign
of human life was the light that burned all night in a
cottage bedroom, here and there; and from garden to
garden went the white owl with that indolent flight
which seems ever about to cease, and he seemed to
be the disembodied soul of a sleeper, vague, homeless,
wandering, softly taking a dim joy in all the misty,
dense forget-me-not, pansy, cornflower, Jacob's ladder,
wallflower, love-in-a-mist, and rose of the borders,
before the day of work once more began.

So I followed the owl across the green and past
the church until I came to the deserted farm. There
the high-porched barn, the doorless stables, the cum-
bered stalls, the decaying house, received something
of life from the owl, from the kind twilight, or from
my working mind. Above the little belfry on the
housetop the flying fox of the weather vane was still,
fixed for ever by old age in the south, recording not
the hateful east, the crude and violent north, the rainy
west wind. Whether because the buildings bore upon
their surfaces the marks of many generations of life,
all harmoniously continuous, or whether because
though dead and useless they yet seemed to enjoy
and could speak to a human spirit, I do not know,
but I could fancy that, unaided, they were capable of
inspiring afresh the idea of immortality to one who

70

desired it. Mosses grew on the old tiles and were like moles for softness and rotundity. A wind that elsewhere made no sound talked meditatively among the timbers. The village Maypole, transported there a generation ago, stood now as a flagstaff in the yard, and had it burst into leaf and flower it would hardly have surprised. Billows of tall, thick nettle, against the walls and in every corner, were a luxuriant emblem of all the old careless ease of the labourers who, despite their sweat and anxiety and hopelessness, yet had time to lean upon their plough or scythe or hoe to watch the hounds or a carriage go by. Tall tansy and fleabane and hawkweeds and dandelions, yellow blossoms, stood for the bright joys of the old life. The campions on the hedge, the fumitory in the kitchen garden, meant the vague moods between sorrow and joy, speaking of them as clearly as when from out of the church flows the litany, charged with the emotion of those who hear it not, though lying near. Had the wise owner admitted these things and for their sake obeyed the command of the will which bade him leave the Green Farm untouched? He might well have done so had he seen the birth of colour after colour in the dawn.

At first, when doves began to coo and late cuckoos to call in invisible woods beyond, I thought that the green of grass was alive again; but that was only because I knew it was grass and could translate its grey. The green trees were still black above a lake of white mist far off when the yellows of hawkweed and tansy rose up. The purple fumitory, the blue of speedwells, came later. And then, as I turned a shadowy corner and came out into the broad half-light just before sunrise, I saw the crimson of innumerable poppies that had a thought of mist pearl enmeshed amongst them.

They were not fifty yards away—they were in a well-known place—and yet there towered high walls and gloomed impassable moats between them and me, such was the strangeness of their beauty. Had they been reported to me from Italy or the East, had I read of them on a supreme poet's page, they could not have been more remote, more inaccessible, more desirable in their serenity. Something in me desired them, might even seem to have long ago possessed and lost them, but when thought followed vision as, alas! it did, I could not understand their importance, their distance from my mind, their desirableness, as of a far-away princess to a troubadour. They were stranger than the high stars, as beautiful as any woman new-born out of summer air, though I could have reaped them all in half an hour. A book in a foreign, unknown language which is known to be full of excellent things is a simple possession and untantalizing compared with these. They proposed impossible dreams of strength, health, wisdom, beauty, passion— could I but relate myself to them more closely than by wonder, as a child to a ship at sea which, after all, he may one day sail in, or of a lover for one whom he may some day attain. I was glad and yet I fatigued myself by a gladness so inhuman. Did men, I asked myself, once upon a time have simply an uplifting of the heart at a sight like this? Or were they destined in the end to come to that—a blissful end? Had I offended against the commonwealth of living things that I was not admitted as an equal to these flowers? Why could they not have vanished and left me with my first vision, instead of staying and repeating that it would be as easy to draw near to the stars as to them?

And yet the mind is glad, if it is troubled, of an impossible, far-away princess. She deceives the mind as Columbus deceived his weary sailors by giving out at the end of each day fewer knots than they had truly travelled, in order that they should not lose courage at the immensity of the voyage.

And still the poppies shone and the blackbird sang from his tower of ivory.

CHAPTER XIV

I HAVE found only two satisfying places in the world in August—the Bodleian Library and a little reedy, willowy pond, where you may enjoy the month perfectly, sitting and being friendly with moorhen and kingfisher and snake, except in the slowly recurring intervals when you catch a tench and cast only mildly envious eyes upon its cool, olive sides. Through the willows I see the hot air quiver in crystal ripples like the points of swords, and sometimes I see a crimson cyclist on a gate. Thus is "fantastic summer's heat" divine. For in August it is right to be cool and at the same time to enjoy the sight and perfume of heat out of doors. In June and July the frosts and east winds of May are so near in memory that they give a satisfaction to the sensation of heat. In September frosts and east winds return. August, in short, is the month of Nature's perfect poise, and I should like to see it represented in painting by a Junonian woman, immobile, passionless, and happy in a cool-leaved wood, and looking neither forward not backward, but within.

Far off I see a forest-covered hill that says "Peace" with a great, quiet voice. From the pool and towards the hill runs a shining road, with some of its curves visible for miles, which I have not followed and dare not follow, because it seems to lead to the Happy Fields.

74

Between the pool and the road is a house built squarely of white stone. A tiled roof, where the light is always mellow as sunset in the various hues that sometimes mix and make old gold, slopes from the many-angled chimneys and juts out beyond and below the wall of the house. In that shadowy pocket of the eaves the martins build, and on a day of diamond air their shadows are as rivulets upon the white wall. Four large windows frame a cool and velvety and impenetrable gloom. Between them stand four still cypresses.

A footpath skirts the pool, and on one side tall grasses rise up, on the other thorns and still more grasses, heavy with flowers and the weight of birds. The grasses almost meet across the path, and a little way ahead mix in a mist through which the white-throat and the dragon-fly climb or descend continually. The little green worlds below the meeting grasses are full of the music of bright insects and the glow of flowers. The long stems ascend in the most perfect grace; pale green, cool, and pleasant to the touch, stately and apparently full of strength, with a certain benignity of shape that is pleasant to the eye and mind. Branched, feathered, and tufted heads of flower top the tall grass, and in the clear air each filament divides itself from the rest as the locks of the river-moss divide on the water's flow. All bend in trembling curves with their own fullness, and the butter-flies crown them from time to time. When wind plays with the perfectly level surface of the grasses their colours close in and part and knit arabesques in the path of the light sand martins. Sometimes the mailed insects creep along the pennons of the grass leaves to sun themselves, other insects visit the forget-me-nots in the pool. Every plant has its miniature dryad.

Nearer, and sometimes in the water, the branched meadow-sweet mingles the foam of its blossom and the profuse verdure of its leaves with willow herb, blue brooklime, white cresses, and the dark purple figwort. A mellow red, like that of autumn oaks or hawthorn at the first touch of spring, tinges the meadow-sweet. The disposition of its flowers is so exquisite that they seem to have been moulded to the shape of some delicate hand; every bud takes part in the effect. The lithe meanders of the stems are contrasted with the intricacy of the goose-grass and the contortion of the forget-me-nots. Both in the midst of the long stalk and in the plume of flowers the branching is so fine and the curves rely so intimately upon one another that a simple copy on paper is cool and pensive after the vanity of cultivated curiousness. Hardly anywhere is there a visible shadow; at most there is a strange tempering of pure light that throws a delicate bloom upon the cattle and the birds, and a kind of seriousness upon the face or flower within its influence. A dark insect of clear wings alights upon the new hawkweed flower, and sits probing deliciously in its deep heart; but, although the petals are in the midst of grasses and under thorns, the fly perches unshadowed, and throws no shade beyond a moistening of the flower's gold. The close purple flowers of the vetches are scarcely duller in the recesses, where the plant begins to climb, than at the summit where the buds bear a fine down. The fish gleam deep in the pool. The dark ivy shines in the innermost parts of the wood.

But these are merely the things that I see beside

the pool, and here, more than anywhere else, the things that are seen are the least important. For they are but the fragments of the things that are embroidered on the hem of a great garment, which gathers the clouds and mountains in its folds; and in the hair of the wearer hang the stars, braided and whorled in patterns too intricate for our eyes. The Junonian woman is a little ivory image of the figure which I think of by the pool. She is older than the pool and the craggy oak at its edge, as old as the stars. But to-day she has taken upon herself the likeness of one who is a girl for lightness and joy, a woman for wisdom, a goddess for calm. Last month she seemed to laugh and dance. Next month she will seem to have grey in her hair. To-day she is perfect.

CHAPTER XV

THE road curves gently but goes almost east and west; on the north side is a bank surmounted by dense thorns; on the south is a low hedge, over which can be seen two broad meadows, with oaks here and there, running up in shining bays among tall woods, and above and beyond those woods several wooded ridges, hunched and blue, on the last of them a windmill like a stag's antlered head that somehow hints at the sea beyond. His back thrust into the northern hedge, an old man leans all the year through, whenever the faint sun draws him forth, or he (as it seems) draws forth the sun, for when the sun is out he is there, and he moves round the curve of the road as the sun moves. Coral-faced, white-haired, he is still straight and tall, though his eyes, that resemble shellfish, seem dissolving in rheum, and his face is stamped with wrinkles like brookside mud where wagtails have played. Apollo, when he disguised himself as an old man, must have looked so. Most of all he loves to lean at the corner from which the windmill is dearliest seen; and thither he looks, though he cannot see it, with a serene satisfaction. For not only did he pass his best manhood close to that hill, but there, as he joyfully recalls, he once climbed an ash tree for a sparrowhawk's nest, and in descending, the miller wrapped a stinging whip about his legs, so that he fell violently and in so doing broke the miller's nose; and that is why he looks towards the windmill affectionately.

What times those were! Wages were low, but then a labourer got many things cheap which others got dear; for the making of a linen smock he paid a woman half a crown, while a farmer had to pay four shillings, and the smocking was the same. Also, in his worst days, if he and his family had nothing on the table but turnip and bread, he had given away two hundred seed potatoes to a man who praised them. Besides, those were the "old-fashioned times" and in fifty or sixty years of toil, suffering and, at length, some leisure, he has proved to himself that they were good. "Some think," said a passer-by to him, "that the old-fashioned times were better than these?"

Think." said he, "I know they were." For surely they were, since it was then that he used to drive a glorious coach twice a week to London and now he does not; and in those days there were" good people" in the little town under the mill, and you knew who they were and their grandfathers too, but who are they now?

And yet, he says, there used to be a great deal less pride. In his young days the farmers and their sons went to church and sang in the choir in their clean white smocks; but now the church is like a gentleman's conservatory. "And, lord! where are the gentlemen now! Many a gentleman looks like an ordinary man about here, and there's many an ordinary man looks like a gentleman. That means a lot of awkwardness for those that care. Now, in the old-fashioned times, we knew a gentleman as soon as we could walk. There was the old squire! He used to expect us to sing carols outside his windows on Christmas Eve I then he would ask us into the hall and give us good mulled ale and a shilling apiece—and how he did give it! Not like a fellow putting a halfpenny into the collection, nor like your good old lady's giving you a pair of gloves too small for you and a tract, as much as to say it is more blessed to give than to receive; but his look was as good as his shilling and made you want to sing, and I believe the old gentleman could no more have done without us than we could do without him."

He is simply a memory with a voice, both of them slightly aided by a present of whisky from an old employer, and in the sun of April he sprouts like any cottager's garden with alyssum and tulips.

Food is a great subject with him, and especially roast pork, from which it is perhaps fair to conclude that it was not often to be had. One bout of it he often recalls. He was still in his prime, a big man of fifty, and though he had been threshing all the morning—"it is a good many ups and downs of the flail to a pound of pork" he says—he had eaten no food and he had none by him and there was none in the house. Presently hunger so far mastered him that he stopped work and took a walk round the farmyard. There he saw a fat pig lying on his side, heavy and making bacon rapidly. In a short time he had laid his plans: lifting up his flail he began to thresh the pig, and shouting above its screams: "Son of a fool, I 'll teach you to eat my dinner." Nor did he cease to beat the pig and to upbraid it for stealing his dinner until the farmer came out and, pitying his case, sent him out a dish of roast pork to make amends. Then he tells a story to celebrate the incomparable joys of such a dish. An old woman had died and two young wives came to lay her out. After doing their work, they sat down on the bed, talking of many matters. Soon they fell to discussing pork. One said that it was best in the middle of the day; the other that it was best at night; and the debate was hot and threatened to be long, when the corpse rose straight up in the bed and said in a gentle voice that it was good at all times, then lay back in peace and never moved again.

But it was wonderful how much could be done without pork. He and two other men had mowed a seven-acre field of grass, all but a bit—and a good crop—in one long day, eating nothing but bread and cheese, and drinking two gallons of new ale apiece. They began at half-past two in the morning, one of them having cleared the edges the night before with an old scythe, because the ground was rough there with sticks and stones. They moved in echelon up the field, he as the strongest mower coming last in the row, so that he could always keep them up to their work; for they had to keep ahead of him lest his swaths should fall over their unmown grass. At five they had the first meal, hardly sitting down to it, for fear of losing time; then again at nine they ate, and so on through the day. The rule for eating and drinking was never to wait until they were really hungry or thirsty, thus avoiding the necessity for a heavy meal and some rest. At first, he said, they talked all the time, especially when they were carrying back their scythes to begin a fresh swath at the bottom of the field; but gradually their talk grew less and less, and they finished in silence at half-past nine. He recalled with pride that when he first mowed barley, being a strong man, he used to take three more drills in his swing than the other man, but in a day's work he had lost ground and he had to give up the conceit.

But he is proudest of his coaching years and especially of one day. It was a very fine April. The snakebirds or wrynecks were screaming all along the road as he set out. The horses were all shining, the white windmills were turning with mad, downward plunges "fit to make you mad." So at the first stop, which was ten minutes, off he went, and sure enough in the first shaw he came to he heard the cuckoo, and as there was a big shallow pond in the heart of the trees, all warm with sun, he stripped and bathed, rejoicing all the time with the thought that he would be able to drive the horses as fast as he liked to make up for the delay. He could have ridden a cow that day. He felt so proud that he wanted to run down some foxhounds that crossed the road before him, and all the way to London the horses' hoofs beat out his name—"Peter Durrant! Peter Durrant!"—as they had never done before. Nowadays, he says, there is not a pair of horses that does not clatter: "Poor pluck to-day! Poor pluck to-day!" which is what a team of plough horses used to sing in his day, as they went home in the afternoon. But so strong is his belief in the old days—to which he belonged—from which he is an exile in a foreign field—that he is never sad as he sits in the sun. He condescends to live on with just such an air as when an old man lays his hand on a boy's shoulder and encourages him. From his conspicuous life he is rather well known, and it happened once that a poet with a command of large margins once made some verses after some misfortune had befallen him and recited them to the old man by the wayside. "That is wonderful," said Peter, "wonder-

ful! How ever did you think of all those things
about a poor old man like me? But 'tis lucky, sir,
that you were not the sufferer, or those beautiful
things would never have been written, for I could
never have thought of them myself."

For the rest, he collects herbs and, with the help of
Culpeper and some little experiment, concocts fragrant
ointments and dark, painful draughts in which a dozen
flavours conflict; nor has he ever killed a man; he
takes them himself. He will bury his nose in a
fragrant posy brought home by the children and say
gravely, and I think with some dark wisdom, "Why,
they must be good for something," and deeply in-
haling, he continues, "At least they are good for old
age." And his own old age he attributes to the diet
of living tadpoles which he used against a decline,
fifty years ago.

CHAPTER XVI

ONE GREEN FIELD

HAPPINESS is not to be pursued, though pleasure may be; but I have long thought that I should recognize happiness could I ever achieve it. It would be health, or at least unthwarted intensity of sensual and mental life, in the midst of beautiful or astonishing things which should give that life full play and banish expectation and recollection. I never achieved it, and am fated to be almost happy in many different circumstances, and on account of my forethought to be contemptuous or even disgusted at what the beneficent designs of chance have brought—refusing, for example, to abandon my nostrils frankly to the "musk and amber" of revenge; or polluting, by the notice of some trivial accident, the remembrance of past things, both bitter and sweet, in the company of an old friend. Wilfully and yet helplessly I coin mere pleasures out of happiness. And yet herein, perhaps, a just judge would declare me to be at least not more foolish than those men who are always pointing out the opportunities and just causes of happiness which others have. Also, the flaw in my happiness which wastes it to a pleasure is in the manner of my looking back at it when it is past. It is as if I had made a great joyous leap over a hedge, and then had looked back and seen that the hedge was but four feet high and not dangerous. Is it perhaps true that those are never happy who know what happiness is? The shadow of it I seem to see every day in entering a little idle field in a sternly luxuriant country.

It is but five grassy acres, and yet as the stile admitting you to it makes you pause—to taste the blackberries or to see how far the bryony has twined—you salute it in a little while as a thing of character. Many of the fields around are bounded by straight-ruled hedges, as if they had been cut up by a tyrant or a slave, with only a few of such irregularities as a stream or a pond may enforce. Not one of the five hedges of this field makes a straight line. The hedge up to your right from the stile is of a noble and fascinating unruliness. So winds a mountain stream down its ladders of crag in Cardigan; into some such form would the edge of a phalanx be worn by long swaying in the height of battle. The other hedges are equally fretted. Here, there is a deep indentation where the cattle lie and wear the blackthorn stems until they are polished for ever; and there the knitted stoles and roots of ash jut out and encroach, fierce and antique and stony, like a strange beast left there to lie in the sweet grass—like a worn effigy over a grave where knight and hound have become mingled in monstrous ambiguity. The surface of the field is of the same wildness. It does not rise and fall in a few sea-like heavings, or in many little waves, nor is it level or in one long, gradual slope, but rising sleepily from west to east it is broken by sudden hollows and mounds. In one place the furze on a mound makes a little world for two or three pairs of linnets and whitethroats, and there are the largest and sweetest blackberries; there also a hundred young stems of brier spend spring and summer in perfecting the curves of their long leaps—curves that are like the gush of water over a dam, and yet crossing in multitudes without crowding, in all ways without discord, like the paths of the flight of swallows when they embroider the twilight air. In another place it is always marshy, the home of marigold and reed. One corner used to be dominated by a tall tented oak, of so majestic balance that when sawn through it stood long in the wind; there the pheasants are proud among bugle or centaury flowers. Here and there a smooth boulder protrudes, guarded by hundreds of blue scabious flowers which welcome butterflies of their own hue, and sometimes a peacock butterfly displays himself on the naked stone.

At the eastern and higher end the field becomes so narrow that it is like a lane, through which the hunt gloriously decants itself among the knolls. It is narrowed still more by a small pond, and round that a tall holly of solid shadow with glancing edges, an oak, an overhanging thicket of bramble and thorn and three old butts of ash, where the fairy gold of toadstools is scattered abundantly, as if sown by one sweep of a generous hand. The pond is the home of one moorhen, which is always either swimming there or hastening to it from the field. It is but as large as a farmhouse kitchen, and yet the moorhen will not desert it, finding the caves among the roots as pleasing as attics to a boy; content with her seeming security though the road passes just above, and rich in her share of sun and moon and stars. To see the moorhen swimming in the narrow pond on a silent and misty autumn morning is to think, now with joy, now with pain, of solitude, but always with a reverie at last that is entangled among the dim, late stars—she possessing the solitary pond, in the solitary autumn country on a planet that is but an element in the solitude of the infinite; and her liquid hoot dwells long in the brain.

It is worth while to watch the pool at dawn, because, though it might seem to be but one of the myriad waters that light candles of adoration and celebration to every dawn, it has then the air, as the mist drips and tingles at the edge, of being a grey priest who has not yet done serving other gods than the dawn, and, until it puts on its white robes and glimmers altogether, it makes with the oak tree a group of pathetic revolt against the day—the oak might be a Saturn or a Lear, the pool in its gradual surrender to the light a Druid sheltering dear and unprosperous mysteries yet a little longer from the proud sun. Then the thrush sings on the holly crest with such blitheness as cannot, nevertheless, excel the water's glory in the fully risen light.

But whatever conversion the little pond undergoes on dawn after dawn, the field as a whole retains the same antiquity, which it announces so powerfully that I knew it on first crossing the stile. Perhaps the lawless shape of the field, its unusual undulations, its unkemptness in the midst of a land all rich with crops—perhaps these things suggested antiquity; but I think not—at least they do not explain it, for it was then strange, and now with all its familiarity it has rather gained than lost its power. It is the same when its outlines are concealed by mist and all I can see is the clover rough with silver dew, white mushrooms, and perhaps one red yolk of maple in the hollow air, and when the snow covers all but the myriad thistles blossoming with blue tits. Enter it in spring—the linnets sprinkle a song like audible sunlight—and yet the field is old. But November is its notable month. Its trees are all oaks and they have hardly lost a leaf; the leaves are falling continually from those smouldering sunset clouds of foliage, which, kingly rich, look as if they would never be poor. One skylark sings high over the field in the rainy sky. The blue rooks unsheathe themselves heavily from the branches and shine silverly and caw with genial voices. A pheasant explodes from a grass tussock underfoot. The air smells like the musky white wild rose; coming from the west it blows gently, laden with all the brown and golden savours of Wales and Devon and Wiltshire and Surrey which I know, and the scent lifts the upper lip so that you snuff deeply as a dog snuffs. A stoat goes with uplifted tail across the field. But the field itself—was there a great house here once and is it dead and yet vocal? Are its undulations and rude edges all that remain of an old wood? Or was there a battle here, and is the turf alive with death? Certainly there is death somewhere speaking eloquently to mortal men. It is not alive, but it laments something, and where there is sorrow there is life.

For just one day in September the goldfinches come and twitter, and are happy among the thistles, and fly away.

CHAPTER XVII

THE BROOK

THE brook rises in a clear, grey, trembling basin at
the foot of a chalk hill, among flowers of lotus and
thyme and eyebright and rest-harrow. Here the stone
curlew drinks, and above is the gently rounded encampment, ancient, and yet still young compared with the
dusky spring which has something gnomish and earthy
about it, though it takes the sun. It drops in thin,
bright links over the chalk, and then for a time loses
its way in playing with cresses and marsh marigolds,
spreading out so finely that hardly will the ladybird
drown that falls therein—falling at length in a cascade
from one dead leaf to another down a hedge bank.
Below, it nourishes the first forget-me-nots, by a
gateway where it slips across the lane, and is dew-fed
by the vetches and clovers that swaddle the posts of
the gate. Now it is unheard and unseen in the
darkness underneath dog's-mercury leaves until it
has gained its first treble voice as, pausing by an
interrupting branch, it fills a hollow and pours over
in icy fingers to the ditch beneath. Here it has cuckoo-
flowers and creeping jenny and butterbur to feed;
thrushes drink of it; beetles dart across it like scullers
that dream now and then upon their sculls. It learns
now to sway the cress, to bow the brooklime, to
brighten the sides of the minnows; the fledgeling of

89

the robin that falls into it dies. It floats the catkin down, and out of it rises the azure dragon-fly. Sometimes it muffles its going in moss, but in a little while it gushes through drains and falls and falls with a now unceasing noise in a land where all the hollows are full of apple trees, rough grey with dewy clover, and through all the hollows winds the brook, dappled by blossom, leaned over by the bee-cradling, sleepy, meadow cranesbill flower; in its green bed the water-voles wear their submerged pathways. Now men have laid a slab of elm or of rude stone across it, and from those they lean to drink at haymaking or harvest; the children float on it pinnaces of bent reed, or set it to turn water-wheels of ash bark, or dip their cans in it for curving minnow or twisting tadpole or the little black circlers that meet and divide and pursue for a few April days. Already it has ranged along its margin rough, leaning willows garlanded by purple ivy; and their leaves that dip to the surface it will never allow to rest. The briers still overleap it in their long dreaming curves. The kingfisher sits over it and the small trout nestle in its bed. It enters many an ash copse and fills it with willow herb and meadow-sweet and all juicy plants, figwort and iris and orchis and hyacinth and reed, with osiers and their mists of crimson and gold. Nymph-like the brook brightens and curves its crystal flesh and waves its emerald hair under the bridges at field corners, where the brambles dip their blossoms, and the nightingale sings and the sedge warbler has its nest. For it the lonely willows in the flat fields shed their yellow leaves most pensively, like maidens casting their bridal garlands off. Three flowering apple trees in one islanded angle on a lawn of perfect grass, a most dream-worthy place, fit for the footprints of the beautiful,

White lope, blithe Helen, and the rest,

seem all its own; for there it first makes a deep sound in falling over a ledge among its own curded, quivering, and moonlit yellow foam. Thereafter it opens wide between broad low banks from which the cattle can step and stand among the reeds under serene tall ashes, and the lily petals float upon it that catch against the branches and against the hearts of men in distant towns. There, too, among the lilies the brook first takes the stars into its heart, but gaily with all its flowers and thick herbage and its rippling fall never still amidst the arrow-headed reed. It moves like the high autumn wain, followed by many children, who have time to leave it and gather flowers and are yet never left behind. The heron comes to it at dawn, knowing from afar the dark pool where it curves under a steep bank and grim oak roots, and slopes down to it solemn and eager and alone in the winter morning. The sand-martin and wagtail often pause in their flight and hover above the placid water and the cool, reflected reeds and water-mint. Where it is all of one depth, between straight banks of cowslip, the boys sit and let their feet waver in the flood and then roll or plunge in, with shouts and gurgling talk, while in the reeds, the dabchick waits with head just above water, trembling for her eggs or cheeping young. On Sunday the country lover, cruel all the week, brings his maid to the brook, and, suddenly tender and a little proud, shows her the moist, weed-covered nest and delights in her melting eyes. Fed now by other brooks, from its own hills and from little woodland springs, the brook consents to spread into a pool in

an old garden, and in the sweet imprisonment of lily
and rose and iris and oleander lies as if asleep, an
indolent Leda contented with the white swan, and
yet escaping all the time, its wild soul rejoicing yonder
beneath the heavily overhanging honeysuckled thorns
of the wide meadows again. Under the white highway
the brook runs and lures men to lean from the parapet
by the milestone and look at the water and take up
some coolness and some bitterness from it when they
return to the blinding miles. Its course is marked by
alders and willows, shaping cornfield and pasture in
divine meanders that seem to have learnt rather to be
contented with travelling than to be eager for the goal.
Could a man but wander in that way once more, like
the child in the field of flowers so multitudinous that
she did not know what to do, but closed her eyes
and was happy yet! Now the otter plays there, and
where the ash roots twist into many a cave. Through
leagues of country the brook runs, passing high, silent
woods and misty, hot, luxuriant, flowering thickets
and wet, cloudy copses full at evening of confused
birds' singing, which no one sees except the brook
and the milk-white heifer who crowns herself in white
roses in the shade as she stands in tall, moist, sump-
tuous angelica and watches her crowned image looking
out of that fair sky in purest waters; then, suddenly
emerging from this lonely country, it falls into a river
and is lost or seems to be lost in the turbid, serious
flow that is soon to know the sea.

CHAPTER XVIII

AN AUTUMN GARDEN

THE cottage gardens are ceremonious and bright with phlox and sunflower and hollyhock; the orchards are yellow with apple, and of all sunburnt hues with plum; in the descending lane you wade in a world of ragwort, knapweed, and Canterbury-bell, with your head in the world of honeysuckle; and, parting the hazel branches to seek their branching clusters, you see now and then in the valley a farmhouse, on whose walls and roofs the hues of fruit and flower all meet harmoniously. They meet as the colours of many pictures meet in some ancient palette, or as Plato and Catullus and Sidney and Shelley meet in some grey schoolmaster.

In every Autumn the farmhouse, with its old tiles and new and its glowing bricks (suppressing easily a few of a putrid blue scattered here and there), seems, in spite of its age, to be a great new flower. It is the royal flower of autumn. It expresses at once all that fruit and flower upon the hill have been expressing laboriously and word by word.

Perfect gay youth and sage antiquity are mingled in the aspect of the house; just as, in an autumn dawn, the gradual veiled golden pomp of serene victory speaks, to one mood, of the happy and mellow antiquity of the world, but, to another mood, speaks of the sublime, insurgent youth which all nights nourish and equip and send forth over the land. In winter it is old; it has apparently been long fortifying itself against the foreign cold of the landscape, snowy white or windy grey. In spring it is old; the green garlands it as in tender mockery. In summer it is old; it is impatient of the bragging rose on its walls and the multiplication of leaf and flower. But in September it is at home, as if after an exile; it remembers only pleasant things—the autumns of two centuries, their harvest, their fruit, their blossom, their hedgerow vintages of bryony and cornel and thorn, their ruddy moons. Gathered about it are the farm-buildings of the same colour, stacks of dark hay, sharp-breasted ricks of corn, maternal, warm oast-houses and orchard and garden, all of the same family.

In the misty days, when no gleam falls from the warm sky on grass or water or fruit, you would say that the sun had stalled his horses for a season within the farmhouse walls; so much they glow; so glorious are they. I have seen the radiant cart-horses coming with grave nods through the farmyard at dawn as if they were to be yoked to the chariot of the sun; the red-haired carter was at least a Phaeton, a son of Apollo, if not Apollo himself.

The garden borders are discreetly furnished, so that they are now as clouds in the neighbourhood of the sun, doing it honour by their liveries. They are populous with sunflowers, hollyhocks (tall, solemn halberds at evening, guarding the outmost edge and held up mysteriously), red-hot pokers rising out of a lake of rose of Sharon and nasturtium, into which run promontories and peninsulas of snapdragon, rocket, Shirley poppy, carnation and phlox of every hue that white and red confederate can invent; here and there fuchsia trees in rivers of autumn crocus, great poppies and evening primrose, and at their feet, like long, coloured shadows stretching away, red flax and pansies and the recurved stonecrop which the tortoise-shell butterfly loves. These bodies of colour change year by year—in one autumn the pansies made a long, curled, purple dragon among all the rest; but always the taller flowers look as if stopped short in the mazes of a dance which is soon to be resumed. Between these two borders are two little lawns divided by a path, whereon the fanciful might see a little beam of the house's influence in the peacock butterfly that returns continually to one stone, settling there as the wanton light cast on ceiling and wall by a raised glass settles when the glass is put down.

It is not a rich or choice garden, though a fitting one. Yet an earlier head of the farmer's family—a student of allegorical prints and emblems, the designer of at least one, in which his own garden had notoriously served as a model for the Eden—was so much enamoured of the flowers and the house that he came, towards the end of his life, to think himself overworldly in his esteem of them, but failed to overcome it, and, a little before his death, in the free wanderings of his mind, announced that he saw Paradise, and that it was even as his garden was, "nasturtiums and all, Jacob" (which was a thrust at the said son, a disliker of those flowers)—except that the vainglorious new carnations were not there.

Travelling beyond the garden, the house declares its lordship over four limes that stand before it, in the home field, at just such a distance that the flying blackbird, frightened from the garden, will stop there instead of going to the hedge beyond. As far as to these trees the house sends out its light and virtue. Approaching them from the hills, the eye of the wayfarer first salutes the outbuildings, the ricks, and the elms; it turns to the house and gratefully pauses there; and last it glides to the limes and is at rest, delighted by that one lyric effort, yet with a slight gravity— even a sigh—at the accomplishment of its sweet toil. Then it is to be seen how noble is the order of the four trees. They are not in circle, square, or line; they make no figure, except that they are in a sharp curve, straightening out as it nears you, so that they have a power as of the first ships of a fleet, coming into sight round a promontory and suggesting majestic numbers. At nightfall the swallows twitter among the topmost branches, sweetly, trippingly, one at a time, or in pairs and companies, for a little while. Suddenly lamps are lit within the house.

CHAPTER XIX

THE immense, solitary, half-veiled autumn land is hissing with the kisses of rain in elms and hedgerows and grass, and underfoot the tunnelled soil gurgles and croaks. Secret and content, as if enjoying a blessed interval of life, are the small reedy pools where the moorhens hoot and nod in the grey water; beautiful the hundred pewits rising in ordered flight as they bereave the grey field and, wheeling over the leagues that seem all their own, presently make another field all a-flower by their alighting; almost happy once more is the tall, weedy mill by the broken water-gates, dying because no man inhabits it, its smooth wooden wheels and shoots and pillars fair and clean still under the red roof, though the wall is half fallen.

And in the heart of this, set in the dense rain, is a farmhouse far from any road; and round it the fields meet with many angles, and the hedges wind to make way, here, for a pond, deep underneath alders; there, for some scattered parcels of hayricks, on a grassy plot, encircling a large walnut tree; and for another pond, beside an apple orchard, whose trunks are lean and old and bent like the ribs of a wreck. A quadrangle of stalls, red tiled, of grey timber—trampled straw in their midst—adjoins the house, which is a red-grey cube, white-windowed, with tall, stout chimneys and steep, auburn roof, and green stonecrop frothing over

97

its porch. In and out goes a rutted, grassy track, lined by decapitated and still-living remains of many ancient elms.

In the overhanging elm branches flicker the straws of the long-past harvest, and the spirits of summers and autumns long past cling to grass and ponds and trees.

The walnut tree among the ricks is dead. Against its craggy bole rest the shafts of a noble, blue wagon that seems coeval with it; long ladders are thrust up among its branches; deep in the brittle herbage underneath it lean or lie broken wheels, a rude wooden roller, the lovely timber of an antique plough, a knotted and rusted chain harrow, and the vast wooden wedge of the snow-plough that cleared the roads when winters were still grim. In the soft, straight rain these things are a buried world, the skeletons of a fair-seeming old life mingled with a sort of pleasant tranquillity as on the calm dim floor of a perilous main.

Half of the fruit trees are dead, save for their lichen and moss and their nests in fork and niche and the robin musing in the branches.

The duck pond, deep below, is all in shadow. The alders lean over it. Some have fallen, and the moorhens have built on them, and the round vole sits there or drops off with the suddenness of fruit; but he cannot dive, for a million dead leaves are sunk or floating in the purple shadows.

Over all is the stillness of after harvest. Long ago the gleaners went home under the frosty moon, and the last wain left its memorial wisps in the elms. The rain possesses all, and a strange, funereal evocation calls up the bronzed corn again, and the heavy wagon and the grim, knitted chests of the bowing horses as they reach the bright-fruited walnut tree. The children laugh and run—who remember it in the workhouse now—and in a corner of the field the reaper slashes hatefully at the last standing rows. The harvest-queen sits on the topmost sheaves. They dance in the barn. Their voices are blithe and sweet; for the rain has washed away their flesh and quieted them now and recalls only golden hours, which linger in this idle autumn place and do not die but only hide themselves, as sunlight hides itself in yellow apples, in red roses, in crystal water, in a woman's eyes.

CHAPTER XX

A GOLDEN AGE

ALMOST at the end of a long walk, and as a small silver sun was leaving a pale and frosty sky, we began to ascend a broad, heaving meadow which was bordered on our right, on its eastern side, by a long, narrow copse of ash trees. At the top of the meadow, hardly a quarter of a mile away, was a little red farmhouse—yet not so little but that it rose with a maternal dignity among and above the sheds and stables, its children, and, like it, of antique red. The home and dependencies gave out a sense of solidity, independence, and seclusion. Our hearts acknowledged at once that it was desirable, saluted it, and were calmly glad at the sight.

At that moment the tumult of a windy day was entirely gone. The north wind now lay dead upon the long white clouds in the east. The smoke from the farmhouse chimneys flowed southward along the top of the ash trees in a narrow, motionless rivulet in the calm air. Far off the hoofs of the returning hunt clattered decently, and combined with the dim memory of the wind in trees and sedge to give to the great meadow an emphasized tranquillity like that which fills an invalid's room when others are just ludibly busy about and below. We walked more and more slowly up the meadow. The red house was clear and hard in the grey air, yet with a richness and implicated shadow as of things submerged. Something which it gave out abundantly filled our minds that had for hours played with casual and untraceable thoughts and images—descended like an enthusiasm among criticisms. In a minute the house was beautiful; it seemed to flower with the happiness of men and women and little children living melodiously; there, we thought, must be minds and bodies which, without carelessness and without stupidity, found in life what some expect from the future and some feign to remember in the past; there was character and beauty and strength, which time flowed over in vain. Hither, it seemed, had drifted upon Lethe's stream all the hopes and wishes and recollections and unaccomplished dreams of unhappy men, and had formed at last a blossoming island in the waste.

And some were enjoying that island now. The very smoke from the chimneys had goodness in it. Even as we walked we turned the moment past into a Golden Age, except that, whenever we looked up towards the house, we knew that all was not yet lost, and that a Golden Age might still succeed the last. Overhead sailed some little rosy clouds that were part of the blossom of that house.

Then suddenly a fearless child ran into the garden and blew a horn and disappeared. Then we knew that the past moments had been as when, in the old tale, men saw an anchor let down out of the clouds and rooted in the ground, and, looking up, saw a rope shaken as if to dislodge the anchor, and heard the voices of sailors aloft in the sky, and then saw a man zlambering down the rope and dying at last, as if tie had been drowned in the air which they breathed easily, and the voices aloft were heard no more.

CHAPTER XXI

I

THE village stands round a triangular, flat green that has delicate sycamores here and there at one side; beneath them spotted cows, or horses, or a family of tramps; and among them the swallows waver. On two sides the houses are close together. The third, beyond the sycamores, is filled by a green hedge, and beyond it an apple orchard on a gentle hill, and in the midst of that a farmhouse and farm-buildings so happily arranged that they look like a tribe of quiet monsters that have crawled out of the sandy soil to sun themselves. There the green woodpecker leaps and laughs in flight. Down each side of the green run yellow roads that cross one another at the angles, two going north, two going south, and one each to the east and west. Along these roads, for a little way, stand isolated cottages, most of them more ancient and odd than those in the heart of the village, as if they had some vagrant blood and could not stay in the neat and tranquil community about the green. Thus, one is built high above the road and is reached by a railed flight of stone steps. The roof of another slopes right to the ground on one side in a long curve, mounded by stonecrop and moss, out of which an elder tree is beginning to grow; and it has a crumbling tiled porch, like an oyster shell in colour and shape.

One has a blank wall facing the road, and into the mortar of it, while it was yet fresh, the workmen have stuck fragments and even complete rounds of old blue and white saucers and plates. In others the mortar is decorated by two strokes of the trowel forming a wedge such as is found on old urns. In the ruinous orchard by a fourth, among nettles and buttercups, there is always a gipsy tent and white linen like blossom on the hedge. One of these houses seems to have strayed on to the green. Years ago someone pitched a tent there, and in course of time put an apple pip into the ground close by and watched it grow. The codling tree is now but a stump, standing at the doorway of a black wooden cottage named after it. Between it and the village pond go the white geese with heads in air.

Off one of those roads the church lifts a dark tower along with four bright ash trees out of a graveyard and meadow which are all buttercups. On three of the others there are plain, square, plastered inns, "The Chequers," "The Black Horse," "The Four Elms," where tramps sit on benches outside, and within the gamekeepers or passing carters sit and wear a little deeper the high curved arm-rests of the settles. But the chief inns stand opposite one another at one corner of the green, "The Windmill," and "The Rose," both of them rosy, half-timbered houses with sign-boards; the one beneath a tall, rocky-based elm which a wood-pigeon loves, the other behind a row of straight, pollarded limes; and opposite them is a pond on the edge of the green. In these inns the wayfarer drinks under the dark seventeenth-century beams; the worn pewter rings almost like glass; moss and ivy and lichen, and flowers in the windows, and human beings with laughter and talk and sighs at parting, decorate the ancient walls. The lime trees run in a line along the whole of one side of the green, and at their feet still creeps a stream where minnows hover and dart, and the black and white wagtail runs. Behind the trees are half the cottages of the village, some isolated among their bean rows and sunflowers, some attached in fantastic unions. Most are of one story, in brick, which the autumn creepers melt into, or in timber and tiles perilously bound together by old ivy; in one the Jacobean windows hint at the manor house of which other memory is gone; all are tiled. Their windows are white-curtained, with geranium or fuchsia or suspended campanula, or full of sweets, and onions, and rope, and tin tankards, and ham, and carrot-shaped tops, dimly seen behind leaded panes. Between the houses and the limes, the gardens are given up to flowers and a path, or they have a row of beehives: in one flower-bed the fragment of a Norman pillar rests quietly among sweet-rocket flowers. Instead of flower gardens, the wheelwright and the blacksmith have wagons, wheels, timber, harrows, coulters, spades, tyres, or fragments, heaped like wreckage on the sea floor, but with fowls and children or a robin amongst them, and perhaps, leaning against the trees, a brave, new wagon painted yellow and red or all blue.

On the other populous side of the green the houses are of the same family, without the limes; except that far back, among its lilac and humming maple foliage and flower, is the vicarage, a red, eighteenth-century house with long, cool, open windows, and a brightness of linen and silver within or the dark glimmer of furniture, and a seldom disturbed dream of lives therein leading "melodious days." Of how many lives the house has voicelessly chronicled the days and nights. It is aware of birth, marriage, death; into the wall is kneaded a record more pleasing than brass. With what meanings the vesperal sunlight slips through the narrow staircase window in autumn, making the witness pause. The moon has an expression proper to the dwellers there alone, nested among the limes or heaving an ivory shoulder above the tower of the church.

From one side to the other the straight starlings fly.

Along the roads go wagons and carts of faggots, or dung, or mangolds in winter; of oak bark in spring; of hay or corn in summer; of fruit or furniture in autumn.

A red calf, with white hind legs and white socks on her forelegs, strays browsing at the edge of the road. A close flock of sheep surges out of the dust and covers the green.

II

We were twelve in the tap of "The Four Elms." Five tramps were on one side; on the other, six pure-blooded labourers who had never seen London, and a seventh. A faggot was burning in the hearth, more for the sake of its joyful sound and perfume than for its heat. The sanded floor, cool and bright, received continually the red hollowed petals that bled from a rose on the table. The pewter glimmered; the ale wedded and unwedded innumerable shades of red and gold as it wavered in the mystic heart of the tankard. The window was held fast, shut by the stems of a Gloire de Dijon rose in bloom, and through it could be seen the gloom of an ocean of ponderous, heaving clouds, with a varying cleft of light between them and the hills which darkened the woods and made the wheat fields luminous.

Now and then a labourer extended his arm, grasped the tankard, slowly bent his arm whilst watching a gleam on the metal, and silently drank, his eyes lifted as if in prayer; then slowly put it back and saw a fresh circle being formed around it by the ale that was spilled.

The tramps leaned on a walnut table, as old as the house, polished so that it seemed to be coated with ice, here and there blackened with the heat transferred to it by a glass bottle standing in the sun. They looked at one another, changed their attitudes and their drinks, gesticulated, argued, swore, and sang. They became silent only when one of their number hammered a tune out of the reluctant piano. They were of several ages and types, of three nationalities, and had different manners and accents. One was a little epicurean Spanish skeleton who loved three things, his own pointed beard, a pot of cider, and the saying of Sancho Panza: "I care more for the little black of the nail of my soul than my whole body." He was a grasshopper in the fields of religion, scandal, and politics, and wore his hat scrupulously on one side. Another was a big, gentle Frenchman, with heavy eyelids, but a fresh boy's laugh. Early in. the evening he scourged the republic; later, he laughed at the monarchy, the consulate, and the empire; and as he went to sleep touched his hat and whispered "Vive la France!" His neighbour was fat, and repeated the Spaniard's remarks when they had been forgotten. It was to be wondered when he walked, what purpose his legs were made to serve. At the inn it was to be seen that they were a necessary addition to the four legs of a chair. He wanted nothing but a seat and not often wanted that. He was, I may say, made to be a sitting rather than a sapient animal, and had been lavishly favoured by Nature with that intention. The fourth, a pale, sour anarchist, hardly ever spoke, but was apparently an honest man, whom his indignant fellows called "parson." The last was one that had been born a poet, but never made one. He sang when he was asked, and later when he was asked not to sing; very quietly and very bitterly he cried when he had sung, indulging in a debauch of despair. Before we parted, the twelfth man sang all the sixteen verses of "Sir Hugh of Lincoln," in the hope of quenching their love of interminable songs. "Heaven and Hell!" said the tramp, "ye make me feel as if I was like Sir Hugh and Lady Helen and the Jew's daughter all in one. Curse ye I bless ye!"

Half-way through the evening the tramps were asleep. The labourers were as they were at the beginning. They sat arow according to age, and nothing but age distinguished them. Their opinions were those of the year in which they were born; for they were of that great family which, at the prime of life or earlier, seems to begin growing backwards, to quote "grandfather" more often, and thus to give the observer a glimpse of the Dark Ages. Life to them was at once as plain and as inexplicable as the patterns on their willow cups or toby jugs. The eldest had a gift of dumbness that sometimes lasted nearly half a century, but once set going and wandering from ploughs to horses, and from horses to the king, his loyalty brought this forth:

"If that Edward wasn't king he ought to be."
Advancing to the subject of hay with a digression
on the church, "Which," said the youngest, "which
came first, parson or hay?"

"What," said the eldest in a short speech that occu-
pied an hour of time, without interruption from the
rest, who drank through his periods and sat watching
him while he drank in the intervals by way of semi-
colon. "What is church for but rector to pray in?
The parson prays for—for a good season, and a good
season means a good hayrick like a church; well, then,
Robert, George, Henry, and Palmston, I say that the
day after they first wanted a rick they put up a church
and put rector in to pray. I," continued he, growing
confident, "remember the Crimea. I had but four
boys then, but bad times they were. But we had
tea, we had tea; the wife used to grate up toast and
pour boiling water on it."

"We called that coffee," said the youngest, a lover
of truth.

As the evening darkened and pipes went out and
the scent of carnations came in with the wind, their
speech became slower, with long intervals, as if they
spoke only after ploughing a furrow. One by one
they seemed to go out like the candles overhead, were
silent, but never slept. The oldest, reddest and
roundest of face, with white hair, looked like the
sun at a mountain crest. The next seemed to be the
spirit of beneficent rain, pale, vague, with moist eyes
and tangled grey beard. The third was as the south
wind, mild, cheerful, pink-faced, with a great rose
in his button-hole. The fourth was the west wind,
that lifts the hay from the level fields into the clouds
at a breath, that robs the harebell of its dew and stores

108

it with rain—a mighty man with head on breast, and small hands united, and flowing hair. And the youngest was the harvest moon, glowing, with close hair and elusive features, a presence as he sat there rather than a man. So they were in the twilight, like a frieze on the white wall.

"Well, us have had fun, haven't us, George?" said the harvest moon. He received no answer as we passed out of "The Four Elms," for all but he had left the world where words are spoken and opinions held; and the hazel lane seemed to be a temple of the mysterious elements that make the harvest and the apple crop and the glory of the hops.

III

Walking in a country churchyard it is often hard to think of it as a place of death. The children play among the tombs. At Easter the village girls bring hither primroses from the woods, planting some, scattering others. Labourers meet and talk there, for the footpaths all converge towards the church. Lovers walk there. The gravedigger is indeed often busy there, but you may go many times and not find him at a grave, and it is seldom but he is planting flowers, pruning bushes, or mowing grass. On the tombs themselves, in epitaph or in lack of epitaph, is written the corporate wisdom of the village, its philosophy and its history half transmuted into poetry. Fancy can never be quiet as the eye, passes from Mary to Rebecca, from John to David, whose record let no one interpret untenderly. I have seen on an afternoon many a novel that shall never be written save as it is written here, deep without gloom, bitter without scandal, on those tablets that have kept their legends too long to be altogether fair. Even the harshest brevity has its fitness, as if it were penned by the right hand of Fate. And here, as in some other matters, we have made an insignificant advance upon our ancestors. The chief records of early races are their tombs. We know not so much that they lived as that they are dead. We guess at their lives from their dead bones. A tool, a weapon, a trinket, a favourite beast, is buried with them, conferring a life in death. In some ancient graves the bodies are found in a sitting posture, and if conjecture be just, we may suppose that the dead man once slept thus and dreamed, daring not to lie down, because no clothes kept off the frost or rain. So the endeavour to provide for an after life by utensils and food has not been wholly in vain. But "Tombs," said the poet, "have their life and death." The headstone is heir to the deceased and out in the world seeks a fortune, which is commonly bad. The fates of tombs have seldom been traced. The history of the epitaph has never been written. Thus is much common philosophy hidden away. Probably no body of literature could be found that is more fertile in homely truth and fancy. But collections of epitaphs either have no plan, or are intended to show only, what is curious, brilliant, or very old.

In this little churchyard a chapter or two of history and progress is easily seen. At the middle of the eighteenth century the sexton wrote the epitaphs, dealing out eulogy and fact with a generous hand. After him came a series of nonentities, whose epitaphs are as like one another as Windsor chairs. Honest regret, or "smiling through tears," was ousted by complacent joy at the celestial lot of the deceased.

Decent friendship was replaced by encomiastic fraud. Like all fashions it was feeble, but like all fashions it had some good; it produced models of accurate expression of "not what he was, but what he should have been." Then in the nineteenth century followed a silent age. "He was alive, and is dead"; tombstones with such inscriptions are like men who do not speak in company, and unlike them, they never disappoint. They say, at any rate, not more than is written of honest men in heaven. The children of those silent people did little but irrelevantly quote or paraphrase the Bible and Dr. Watts. The epitaphs were now thought worthy of a clear, large type; the fashion at least taught the children to spell. Some there were who gained no small village reputation by a diligent study of these sentences. Even the wiser pillars of the village, whether they could read or not, were sure of awe and admiration among their audience, if their speeches—political, religious, or scandalous— were launched by "As the great Dr. Watts wrote . . ." or "In the words of Amos, whom you may know . . ." Not of this period, but first notorious then, was the epitaph on Sir——, Bart. His family being still one of splendour and influence, everything connected with it was held in esteem. It was, therefore, not unnatural that the admirers of an aged spinster should put upon her tomb the epitaph that was picked out with letters of gold on that of the young baronet:

The good die young.

Strangers are apt to wonder first at the longevity common in the parish—then at the humour of the thing—and go away both contented and deceived. For some time it was not uncommon to quote a grave passage from Shakespeare, with decent omission of the author's name; when, however, a revolutionist not only published "Shakespeare" on a headstone, but "Romeo and Juliet" too, the vicar was approached, the sexton ran a risk every day, the innkeeper, the J.P. was approached. The bereaved person had in the meantime erased the offending words, and until recently you might read:

> God rest his soul! He was a merry man,

beneath which the curious eye may still discover "Kings iii," placed there in homage to parish prejudice. The storm almost raised by the introduction of two lines by Robert Burns—"a poet as well as a drunkard," according to village rumour—is still remembered. The parish clerk having doubted whether it was in "Ancient and Modern," took refuge in the book of Ecdesiastes, until a confidant (a fearless thinker and a friend of Chartists) swore it was written by a lord. The vicar was questioned. Opening a book whose cover was well known to the doubter, and repeating with nasal unction the offending words, he drew tears and apologies from the man. After that comparative freedom of choice was enjoyed, and some went bravely back to

> Afflictions sore long years I bore,

as recently as 1885. Tennyson was in favour at that time; no one grumbled since he was the author of

> That good man, the clergyman.

But when I brush aside the leaves and flowers of herb honesty, growing by the older graves, although I am willing to admit that the village view of death has become more solemn, I cannot but wish back again the author of

> This world has lost old John the sexton,
> What business has he in the next one?

Where are the robuster views of which this is a late reminder? The gay, the fanciful, the calmly elaborate epitaphs seem to have gone for ever, and in the newer portion of the churchyard it is hard not to think of death, unless we turn to the unnamed little mounds that rise and fall like summer waters, so calm, so soft, so green, that fancy cannot make them aught save pillows for the weary. I have seen a tramp sleeping there and envied him his unconscious return to the good old insouciance which was warm with the thought that in the midst of death we are yet alive.

IV

From the churchyard run twelve footpaths; some ending at farmhouses close by; some losing themselves in the nearest road; one leading nowhere, nor of any use to-day, since the house which drew it thither across the wheat is under the cow-parsley and grass; one going on without end, touching here and there a farmhouse, crossing a road, passing in at the door of an inn and out through the garden, as if some friendly man had made the path by following his heart's desire. Most of the paths lead up on to the hills among which the village is set. From the highest part, in spring, the warmth and life of the scene below contrast strangely with its immense age, as the new brazen leaves of the oak with their ancient trunk. The houses are old, the church older, the farm wall yonder is partly the remains of a castle of Norman date. The hedges twist so fantastically because they also are old, marking ancient paths, the edges of departed woods, the gradually advancing line of men's camp fires overcoming the wilderness. In that hollow the gemote used to sit. Here a company of cavalry charged down the hill and to a man went over the chalk pit to the road and to death. There stood an abbey, now speaking only through a curve added to the undulations of the land. In the next village a poet was born. A dolmen rises out of the wheat in one field, like a quotation from an unknown language in the fair page of a book. The names of the places are in the same language, and yet how smoothly they issue from the lips. The little roads, so old, wind among the fields timidly, as if they marked the path of one creeping with difficulty through forest coeval with the world. Some roads have disappeared —there where the wheat grows thin in a narrow band across the field. Another is disappearing; worn to the depth of some feet below the surrounding fields by the feet of adventurers, lovers, exiles, plain endurers of life, its end is to become a groove full of hazels and birds, the innermost kernel of the land, because nobody owns and nobody uses it. In contrast with those, how certain of its aim the great road running east and west, the road of conqueror, pilgrim, merchant, the embodiment of will and opportunity; and that, too, so old that heron and rook seem to recognize it as they go over at nightfall. There is no age that does not play its part in the symphony of this June scene. And yet, standing still upon the ridge commanding it, when the roads are overhung by the blithe new green of beech leaves and paved with their ruddy chaff, these things become a part of the silence and clear air which they trouble and enrich as do the storied pavements and walls of a cathedral, thrilling the ear and shaming the powers of the eye, so that in the end the mind vibrates with the strangely inter-woven melodies of joy in the life that still triumphs within us, and of acquiescence in the death which will leave of us not so much trace as can add to the silence and clear air one tone audible to mortal men.

CHAPTER XXII

In November I returned for a day to a lonely cottage which I had known in the summer; and all its poppies were gone. Here and there, in the garden, could be found a violet, a primrose, a wood sorrel, flowering; the forget-me-nots and columbines had multiplied and their leaves were dense in the borders; the broad row of cabbages gleamed blue in a brief angry light after rain; the black-currant leaves were of pure, translucent amber at the ends of the branches. In the little copses the oaks made golden islands in the lakes of leafless ash, and the world was very little in a lasting mist.

Yet it was not impossible to reach greedily ahead to spring, and I was doing so, in spite of the incredibly early fall of night amid the whirling and crying of lapwings, when, suddenly, a dead elm tree spoke of the summer that was past. Dead, it had been worn by the summer landscape as a memorial, as a "reminiscential amulet." It alone was now still the same, and strangely it spoke of the summer which it had not shared; and I recalled swiftly a night and daybreak of July.

All night we had sat silent with our books. There was no other company within a mile save that of the tall clock, with a face like a harvest moon, which did not tick, but stood silent with hands together pointing at twelve o'clock, seeming to rest, and to be content with resting, at the tranquil and many-thoughted midnight which it had so often celebrated alone until we came. But we were glad of the clock. It allowed us to measure the rich summer night only by the changing enchantments of Burton's and Cervantes' and Hudson's page, and by the increasing depth of the silence which the owl and restless lapwing broke no more than one red ship breaks the purple of a wide sea. It is a commonplace that each one of us is alone, that every piece of ground where a man stands is a desert island with footprints of unknown creatures all round its shore. Once or twice in a life we cry out that we know the footprints; we even see the boats of the strangers putting out from the shore; we detect a neighbouring island through the haze, and creatures of like bearing to ourselves moving there. On that night a high tide had washed every footprint away, and we were satisfied, raising not a languid telescope to the horizon, nor even studying the sands at our feet.

Not less strangely or sweetly than it creeps in among dreams, came in the whisper of the first swallows of the dawn among our books; and Cleopatra, the cat, slipped out through the window and left me.

But it happened that I rose and drew a curtain aside to see whether she went to the woods or to the barn. The night was over. The pool at the bottom of the garden was glazed and dim and slightly crumpled, like the eye of a dead bird; and all its willows were grim.

In the garden there was a bee. A little wind broke up the poppies petal by petal, so that they vanished like fair children in the midst of their perfections— cut off, and marked in the memory chiefly by the blank they leave, and not by an abundance such as older people entail upon us to mimic life. Hardly had I ceased to watch them than it was day. The cattle in a distant meadow stood still at the edge of their own shadows as if at the edges of pools. The dead elm tree seemed but a skull-capped, foolish jester who set a sharper edge upon our appetite for summer and the sun. The corn, the woods, rejoiced. The green woodpecker laughed and shone in his flight, which undulated as if he had been crossing invisible hedges. A south-west wind arose and rain fell softly, yet not so soothingly but that an odd thought thrust itself into my mind.

I thought of how Cervantes was not enjoying it, and in a moment I saw him and Burton and Wordsworth and Charles Lamb close by, crouching and grey, as if they had been buried alive, under knotted cables of oak root, deep under the earth which was then bearing carnation and wild rose. The wind found out the dead elm tree and took counsel in its branches and moaned, although the broad light now reigned steadfastly over leagues of shining fields.

CHAPTER XXIII

THE PRIDE OF THE MORNING

THE sun has been up for an hour without impediment, but the meadows are rough silver under a mist after last night's frost. The greens in cottage gardens are of a bright, cold hue between blue and grey, which is fitter for the armour of heaven, or the landscape of some strong mystic, than for one who loathes to leave his bed. The blackbirds are scattering the frost, and they live in glittering little hazes while they flutter in the grass.

But the sky is of an eager, luminous pale blue that speaks of health and impetuousness and success. Across it, low down, lie pure white clouds, preserving, though motionless, many torn and tumultuous forms; they have sharp edges against the blue and invade it with daggers of the same white; they are as vivid in their place in that eager sky as yews on a pale, bright lawn, or as lightning in blue night. If pure and hale intelligence could be visibly expressed,' it would be like that. The eyes of the wayfarer at once either dilate in an effort for a moment at least to be equal in beauty with the white and blue, clear sky, or they grow dim with dejection at the impossibility. The brain also dilates and takes deep breaths of life, and casts out stale thought and coddled emotion. It scorns afterthought as the winds are flouting the penitent half-moon.

A squadron of wild fowl races through the crystal

air; the mind expands with their speed, and tries to share it, and believes that it succeeds. A heron goes over solemnly, high up, and as if upon some starry business in that profound, bright air; the mind at once attunes itself to that majesty and directness and simplicity:

> And each imagined pinnacle and steep
> Of godlike hardship.

A starling sits on the weathercock with ruffled feathers, watching the sky with one eye and then with the other, and his form and voice are sharp and pure as they joyfully pierce the air. The weather-cock itself shines like Mars. Together, they speak of the cold and vigour and health and beauty which abide somewhere in the sky to-day and not inaccessibly.

High above me, here and there upon the road, stand oast-houses, with their conical roofs ruddy against the sky, and over them the newly painted white cowls point eastward, and in their whiteness seem to have been set as a signal to say that it is the west wind after frost that has made the world what it is; they point out a road which, if I could follow it, would lead to the very court of mind and beauty, yonder, afar off, where the wind and the heron and the wild ducks are going. There I might learn to realize the long, joyous curves in which thought and action and life itself sweep onward to their triumphs. . . .

But I know well that long hopes and wide, vaulting thoughts are not usually nourished by lane and foot-path and highway, on and on; and probably I shall stop at "The Black Horse" over the next hill, where a man may always lighten his burden on a Tuesday by hearing the price of beasts.

CHAPTER XXIV

THE METAMORPHOSIS

As the sun rose I watched a proud ash tree shedding its leaves after a night of frost. It let them go by threes and tens and twenties; very rarely, with little intervals, only one at a time; once or twice a hundred in one flight. Leaflet—for they fall by leaflets—and stalk twirled through the windless air as if they would have liked to fall not quite so rapidly as their companions to that brown and shining and oblivious carpet below. A gentle wind arose from the north and the leaves all went sloping in larger companies to the ground—falling, falling, whispering as they joined the fallen, they fell for a longer time than a poppy spends in opening and shedding its husk in June. But soon only two leaves were left vibrating. In a little while they also, both together, made the leap, twinkling for a short space and then shadowed and lastly bright and silent on the grass. Then the tree stood up entirely bereaved and without a voice, in the silver light of the morning that was still young, and wrote once more its grief in complicated scribble upon a sky of intolerably lustrous pearl.

But by the next day the grief was healed, for what was clearest about its branches was the swiftness and downward rushing and curving flight which they suggested—as of birds stooping in lines to their tree-top nests—as of divers at the moment when their descent mingles with their ascent—as of winged Greek gods and goddesses slanting to earth with wave-like breasts.

CHAPTER XXV

I

THEIR house is a small russet cave of three dim
compartments—part of a farmhouse, the rest having
fallen to ruin, and from human hands to the starlings,
the sparrows, and the rats. No one will live in it
again. Inside, it is held together by the solid poetry
of their lives, by gay-coloured, cheerful, tradesmen's
pictures of well-dressed children and blooming horse-
women, and the dogs of gentlemen, memorial cards
of the dead, a few photographs, some picture post-
cards pasted over flaws in the wall, and the worn
furniture of several disconnected generations. The old
man's tools in the kitchen are noble—the heavy
wrought-iron, two-toothed hoe, that falls pleasantly
upon the hard clay and splits it without effort and
without jarring the hand, its ash handle worn thin
where his hand has glided at work, a hand that nothing will wear smooth; the glittering, yellow-handled
spades and forks; the disused shovel with which he
boasts regretfully that he could dig his garden when
he lived on deep loam in a richer country than this;
and still the useless "hop-idgit" of six tynes—the
Sussex "shim"—which he retains to remind others,
and perhaps himself, that he was a farmer once.
He had twenty or thirty acres and a few cows. The
cows all died in one year and he became a labourer.

His wife remembers those days. She was a tall woman and stooped at the doorway thatch; now she cannot rise to it. For every day she went many times to the sweet brook, a quarter of a mile away, rather than take the grey liquor of the pond for her cows. That is how she came to be bent like an oak branch on which children swing, or like a thorn that knows the west wind on the hill or the shore. Now she cannot carry a pail, for it would sweep the ground. She cannot see the apples in autumn until they have fallen to her feet. Her flesh seems to have assumed an animal sweetness, for her bees will cluster on the brown hands. Birds and beasts take to her as to an old tree, though she has pity for them but no love. Sometimes as she sits at her door the robins come fearlessly close to her—hedge-sparrows too, if there is nobody else near, and even the partridges that come for the ants in the old dock roots. She watches them with her dull eye and seems easily to have found a Franciscan friendliness when, as if angry with the creatures for seeing her frailty, she stamps her feet and drives them away. Then she relents and tries her power, as if she has half persuaded herself that it is a happy talent. She will crush a mouse in her fingers, and yet they still run over her in their merry business night or day, as they would over a tree that had fallen, and proved fatal to some of them in its death. Yet, in spite of her apparent indifference, I think that she knows the animals more than we who patronize them. Left alone with a cat, she shows, indeed, none of the endearments of a civilized woman, but quietly concedes and demands concessions, very much as when a horse and some cows are sheltering from the heat together in a limited shade.

She speaks hardly ever, except with animals. But in church her lips move long after others are tired of "have mercy upon us."

"Lord!" she says, "you are very kind, but your children are very many. All the sparrows in my garden have to be tended, and I suppose the mice, the moles, the worms, the lizards, the shining things that run and fly and crawl, and all the flowers, trees, and birds. Oh! Lord, I had seventeen children and among so many you seemed not to. notice some, and they died just anyhow in their happiness, and perhaps then you have forgotten me altogether, and I shall not even be taken away. I have heard that the good shall prosper. You have said it yourself. But I know not what is good or what is prosperity. For what am I? I am willing to learn, yet I am not taught. Am I good? Am I prospering? Lord! what am I to do? There are thousands and thousands of strong and rich and beautiful and happy things in the world, but as for me, I seem to crawl about among them in darkness like a mole. Nevertheless, glory to God the father, Lord of all, though you have done some things that I would not have done, and as to the weather . . . but I know not your designs. Glory to the Son though he has long been dead, he was a good man. Glory to the Holy Ghost, which I do believe in, though they say there are no ghosts really. I am a poor old woman, born in Scotland, and a Scotswoman still. My name is Margaret Helen Page, and I live at the Hoath Cottage in the wood, at the end of the lane, where you turn up by 'The Blue Anchor,' in going to Horsmonden. There I shall abide and am to be found there, except on Sunday evening in fine weather, when I come to this holy place. Oh, come,

Lord, when you have looked after all the sparrows, some day, and take me."

"If," she said once, "if God's a Christian man, I do not know what he means by this weather."

"I reckon he manages about as well as could be expected in such a funny world," replied her husband. "Remember old Farmer King who used to swear at the weather so. One day when he had got his hay dry at last and saw it coming on to rain, he picks up a handful and stuffs it into his pocket, and says he will carry that much home dry at any rate, but if he didn't fall into the brook on his way back and get wet to the skin. Such are the ways of God."

But she was not convinced, for, with all her feebleness of body and conversation, she proves that man is older than Christ and Buddha, than Jehovah and Jupiter, and that not even such presences on the earth have left behind footpaths in which he can wander in security. She compels us to realize, if we have not done so before, that if we could isolate the child of Christian parents on a solitary island away from all religious influences, he would grow into something curiously different from a Christian, and something marvellously ancient too. Her language, stripped of its tattered and scanty Christianisms, and her acts, without that Sunday journey, reveal the multitude's eternal paganism, which religions ruffle and sink into again—the paganism of the long-lived, most helpless, proudest and loneliest of animals, contending with winter and bad weather, with accident and disease and strange fears; rejoicing in fine weather, in strength, in the appetites; hating decay; distrusting the inhumanity of the heavens and animals and men from other climates; uncertain, troubled, and thinking

little, about the future. For her the world is a flat
place, decorated with a pattern of familiar and other
fields, with hills, rivers, houses, a sea, a London, a
Highland valley of children and old-fashioned ways,
and infinitely far off towards the sunset, lands of
tigers, monkeys, snakes, strange trees and flowers and
men, with earthquakes, volcanoes, huge storms, all lit
by sun and moon and stars—and a heaven also and a hell.
Very real to her is the snow and the thaw drip from
the roof, the dry heat of summer, the apple blossom,
the coming of the swallows, the growth of carrots,
potatoes, cabbages, and weeds, the coming home of
her husband sober or drunk, the use of a few silver
coins week by week, the announcement that old Mrs.
Fuller is dead or that Mrs. Rixon has another child,
the cold at four o'clock on a January morning and
the warm th all night in July as she sits sleeping,
because of her doubled back, like the corpse of a
caveman in his grave, the endlessness of days when
she is alone and has nothing to do but to remember
and try to remember. She has no hopes, no purposes.
I have seen her picking up oak branches in May
after the fall of the great trees, and she will go on
after her arms are filled, adding to the pile from above,
and at the same time losing others from the sides,
until at last it is dark and she goes home. Even so
she does in life, accumulating memories and affairs;
and letting them fall, until the end. Yet is it a little
hard that there should be no kindly god or goddess to
deceive her and receive her prayers and sanctify her little
unnecessary acts, that the very wood at night, round
about the house, is merely dark and full of sounds
and no home for her. The beautiful Jewish stories
told to her by clergymen of some birth and education,

though she will gladly listen to them, are little better than ribands for oak faggots—for, though a Pagan, she has no gods. The gods of this part of the earth have long been hurled into Tartarus and bolted there in that grotesque company which the prophets of the ages have gathered together. And so she goes through life, like a child in a many-windowed house, looking on sea and barren land, and full of corridors, resounding and silent by hours, with dim, enormous apartments, bolted doors, and here and there a picture, a skeleton, an old toy, a reminiscent voice. . . .

II

Compared with Margaret Helen Page, her husband, Robert, is a citizen of the world. He knows all the farmers in the neighbourhood, thatching for one, hay-making for another, gardening, woodcutting, washing, or pole-pulling in the hop-garden for others. He can even make the beautiful, five-barred gates, with their noble top bars, tapered and shaped like a gunstock and barrel. All the inns are known to him, and the labourers and wayfaring men who resort to them. He will gossip, and the rich do not disdain to listen to the fabrications and selections which he mixes charmingly for them alone. The workhouse or death is not more than a few years ahead of him; for he stoops with difficulty and will make haste for no man; yet he will cheerfully quarrel with a farmer in the middle of the winter, pick up his coat, take his wages, and go off to the inn and drink all that he has; if the farmer grumbles in September that Robert has been taking merely an honest bushel of hops from the pickers, he will not give way to the extent of a handful. No one can thatch as he can. His tall haystacks look like churches when they are new, and so they remain. The roofs of his cornricks are shaped like breasts, with convex curves that make the same lines against the sky as you walk round. His vegetable plots are invariably as flat as lawns, their sides evenly sloping to the paths. He stops in the midst of his work and smokes and thinks; and he expects to be paid for his thinking. In the spring he catches moles, hanging them up on the briers or thorns with great care, twisting the twigs round them so that they stay until fur and bone are indistinguishable and break up into dust.

At the inns he hears the gossip of the universe, heaping up as in a marine store the details of murders, swindles, divorces, expensive pictures of Venus, etc., horse races, cricket matches, letters from archbishops and literary men, distant wars, new foods and diseases and cures, automobiles, the cost of rich men's dinners, how to live happily, the extravagance of the poor, how to feed on a shilling a week. These things are "in print" and therefore true. But he utters no opinions of his own. He consents to exchange his recollections and to accept others; then he sinks into the happy silence of those who have not the gift of ratiocination. What dark, undisturbed depths of personality are his—immense depths yielding to the upper world, now and then, an ejaculation, as Gilbert White's well yielded a black lizard at times.

"I wonder," he ejaculated once, "I wonder what God did with himself before he made such a kettle of fish as this world."

Again, "Now supposing that all these things in the

Bible about Adam and the beginning had never been written down, and we had not been told that God did it, what should we have done? Should we have found out these things for ourselves?"

Once he related a dream:

"Sometimes when I am all alone, and my old girl says the same, it seems to me that I am not of much account; it is as if I had been forgotten and left off the register, and how will it be at the Judgment Day? Sometimes I think to myself, It will be fine sleeping and never hearing the blessed trumpet and getting into that crowd. But one night I dreamed that I had died and was up above, and that an angel woke me up and asked me to take his trumpet, because he wanted a bit of sleeping after waiting ever since Adam 's time, and I was to blow it at twelve o'clock and then it would be Judgment Day. Well, as he looked like a gentleman, I said I would, and I took the trumpet and stared at it a bit, because it was that trumpet that was to wake the dead for the Judgment Day. I was wide awake and I could see the dead all round me, more of them than there are mangolds in twenty acres. Close to me were the angels, and they were all asleep, worn out with waiting so long, I suppose. They had wings like peacocks and owls and orpingtons—beautiful! I enjoyed myself. But when it got near to twelve o'clock I got a bit anxious. The angel was fast asleep and I did not see why I should wake him up, or anybody else. Once or twice I put the trumpet to my lips, but I thought—No, I would sleep myself and there would be no Judgment Day. But I could not sleep for thinking of the keeper who used to kill my old girl's cats as fast as they grew up and went into the woods at night; and, without thinking what I was at, I blew the trumpet and what with the terrible noise and the sight of all these poor people waking up I awoke myself, and my old girl said that I had made a noise like a trumpet in my sleep. But it did seem a pity that they should all wake up just as if they had to go to ploughing and all that again."

But Bacchus is his only god, who has already given him many gifts. On Friday nights he is as a child upon the throne, holding himself wonderfully straight on the settle at the inn, never letting go of the tankard except to have it filled, and smiling delicately with weary eyes, as he drinks the six ale—

> Much more of price and of more gratious powre
> Is this, then that same water of Ardenne,
> The which Rinaldo drunck in happie howre,
> Described by that famous Tuscane penne:
> For that had might to change the hearts of men
> From love to hate, a change of evil choise:
> But this doth hatred make in love to brenne,
> And heavy heart with comfort doth rejoyce.
> Who would not to this vertue rather yceld his voice?

At such times he speaks little, except a few words of nonsense to strangers who come in; but he smiles continually, as if he had forgiven all things, and even as if he silently preached forgiveness to all the world. His tenderness to children and animals is wonderful. He would pass for a saint, an angelic doctor, or even something higher. To some, indeed, he might seem to be the original from which field artists have every- where modelled the scarecrow. The young men recog- nize the resemblance and smile. The older men per- haps see in him an apotheosis of themselves, more twisted, more starved, greener in the hat and coat, and they do not smile. He has a lean, acorn-coloured face, adorned with relenting blue eyes, small hawk nose, clear-cut shrivelled lips and chin, and fresh brown hair hanging like a lion skin over his head and neck, and curling sumptuously.

I can fancy him a lesser god in some mythology. To him come the weak and ashamed; the shamefaced female tramp who went hungry, having asked for a direction to Maidstone instead of for food, because the farmer's voice was hard and he was young and strong and her skirt was old and her breast shrunken; and he who looked through the hedge at some fair children playing, and then, because one of them screamed at catching sight of him in searching for a nest, raised a hideous cry and sent them terrified away; the curst, scandalous lean maid who melts with momentary tenderness over her starved and piebald cat, and calls him "Prettiest"; all such as are foolish and slow of thought and slower of speech, and laugh at what they love because others do and then weep in solitude; those who, unable to care for anything much, grow ardent in a simulated affection and blush when a cruel strong one finds them out; those who know not what they desire except a little tranquillity before the end and know that they shall not obtain it; the drunken and obscene who are without graces, but also without repentance; those who vainly complain and fret about the evils which they have deserved and cannot endure; those who cannot keep up with life because of one beautiful or terrible thing in the past; those who mourn, they know not why; the little base ones who admire good and lovely things, and fear to hurt them by approval. And they should come to this god, Robert, as one in whom each saw his little unknown virtue and should be lifted up thereat. They should bring to his altars sour bread and rotten flesh and fruit fallen before its time, and worn-out, shattered things; and his priests, leprous, and scrofulous, and squint-eyed all, should rejoice then and tell the worshippers to be no more cast down, because in this, their god, were to be found all their little virtues, and behold! he endured for ever and looked upon them pitifully and interceded continually with the high gods. Then would they drink until they were thoroughly drunken, and the god would tell them that death came soon, and that their sleep would be heavier than they could dream of, for no king, or judge, or policeman, or clergyman, could ever disturb their sleep, though armed with sharpest swords and most cruel words.

CHAPTER XXVI

NOVEMBER RAIN

CLOSE, perpendicular, quiet rain came upon me when
I was ten miles from last night's shelter and ten
miles from my end. Shelter was not near, nor indeed
to be thought of in an untrodden lane which had
been, for some time, and seemed to go on for ever,
winding through the delicious, vacant country of a
late autumn Sunday, while it was yet early in the
day and yet not so early but that the milking was
over, and the milk carts gone, and the cattle satisfied
and slow after their first questing in the fields. The
rain was so dense, and the light so restrained, and
the drops hung so about my eyes, and the sound
and the sweetness of it made my brain so well contented with all that umber country asleep, that what
I saw was little compared with what reached me by
touch and by darker channels still. I rarely see much
in the country—a few herbs underfoot, the next field,
the horizon woods, some brief light that shows only
its departing hem; for, like others, I always carry out
into the fields a vast baggage of prejudices from books
and strong characters whom I have met. My going
forth, although simple enough to the eye, is truly as
pompous as that of a rajah who goes through the jungle
on a tall and richly encrusted elephant, with a great
retinue, and much ceremony and noise. As he
frightens bird and beast, and tramples on herb and
grass, so I scatter from my path many things which

are lying in wait for a discoverer. There is no elephant more heavy-footed and no rifle more shattering than the egoism of an imitative brain. And thus the little thing I saw was an unusual discovery.

It was a triangular, six-acre wood below me, across a bare and soaking ploughland. The wood was mainly of ash and the myriad stems were a grey mist, only denser and a little clearer than the rain itself. Out of them rose half a hundred oaks which were exuberant in foliage of hues so vigorous and splendid in their purple that it was impossible to think of it as on the edge of death, but easy to think of it as in a deathless prime. One thrush sang heartily somewhere deep among the ash trees, and that was the only sound, for the sound of the rain was but a carpet on which that song walked forth, delicate-footed, haughty, and beautiful. . . .

When I had walked another mile, the wood was out of sight, the thrush unheard. The wood is now purple immortally, for ever that song emerges from its heart, as free from change as one whom we remember vividly in the tip-toe of his exulting youth, and dying then has escaped huskiness, and a stoop, and foul breath, and a steady view of life.

CHAPTER XXVII

It is a quiet valley in which moist fields of meadow, mowing grass, mangold, and stubble are bounded from one another by deep ditches and good hedges of maple, thorn, and hazel, with here and there an oak, or by oak woods that rise above an undergrowth of grey ash. Every half-mile there is a tiled farmhouse with low-pitched roof and low, square windows, their frames painted white, and between them rose trees climbing; in the gardens of most, two plots of lawn are surrounded by rich dark borders and divided by a path; and each has a careless shrubbery of Portuguese laurel, lilac, syringa, and elder, hardly cut off from the orchard that grows as it will above grey rank grass, and close by at least two ponds. One little stream winds through the valley and gains at times much glory of speed and sound and foam from the rain off the hillside. A few grey, smooth roads cross the valley.

It is January, and the predominant grass is green and shining in the sun. The rusty oaks and the farmhouse roofs glow. The bare clean hedges glitter with all their stems of olive hazel, silver oak and ash and whitethorn, and blackthorn ruddy where the cattle have rubbed. A lark rises and sings. A flock of linnets scatters and drops little notes like a rain of singing dew, and over all is a high blue sky, across which the west wind sets a fleet of bright white clouds to sail; into this blue sky the woods of the horizon drive their black teeth.

In the immense crystal spaces of fine windy air thus bounded by blue sky, black woods, and green grass, the jackdaws play. They soar, they float, they dance, and they dive and carve sudden magnificent precipices in the air, crying all the time with sharp, joyous cries that are in harmony with the great heights and the dashing wind. The carter's boy raises his head from the furrow and shouts to them now and then, while the brass furnishings of his horses gleam, their shoulders grow proud and their black tails stream out above the blue furrow and the silver plough.

Suddenly a pheasant is hurled out of a neighbouring copse; something crosses the road; and out over a large and shining meadow goes a fox, tall and red, going easily as if he sailed in the wind. He crosses that meadow, then another, and he is half a mile away before a loud halloo sounds in the third field, and a mile away before the first hound crosses the road upon his scent.

Run hard, hounds, and drown the jackdaws' calling with your concerted voices. It is good to see your long swift train across the meadow and away, away; on such a day a man would give everything to run like that. Run hard, fox, and may you escape, for it would not be well to die on such a day, unless you could perchance first set your fair teeth into the throats of the foolish ones who now break through the hedge on great horses and pursue you—I know not why— ignorant of the command that has gone forth from the heart of this high blue heaven, Be beautiful and enjoy and live!

CHAPTER XXVIII

THE BARGE

SPRING and summer and autumn had come—flowing into one another with that secrecy which, as in the periods of our life, spares us the pain of the irretraceable step—and still a golden tree stood here and there in the hollowed lawns. . . . Snow fell on singing thrushes and golden trees, and when it was over a half-moon of untouched grass under a dense hawthorn was as a green shadow on the white land. . . . Then the year paused; there was a swallow still here and there; but again there was snow. . . .

The world had been black and white for many days. The cygnet-coloured sky had been low from dawn to sunset; rarely a cloud dimly appeared in it, seen and lost and seen again, like a slow fish in rippling water. By night the iron firmament had been immense and remote.

Out of doors, as we walked, it was a source of faint satisfaction that we were clothed and fed; and it was easy to think of a less happy condition. We were in a primitive world. In those short days the world seemed to have grown larger; distance was more terrible. A friend living thirty miles off seemed inaccessible in the snow. The earth had to be explored, discovered, and mapped again; it was as it had been centuries ago, and progress was not very real to our minds. Only when we saw a great fire at an inn, a red face or two, a copper vessel thrust in among the coals to warm the ale, did there appear to be much being done to fight winter and to subjugate this primitive world. We saw the birds around us for what they were—little, tender, hungry things, entirely sorrowful, easily killed, and not mere melodious attendants upon our delight.

A train crawling along the valley at a distance was very feeble in our eyes. The strength and purpose were concerted. It was like a thought which is without the implements for action—pathetic and impotent, it was absorbed easily by the vast white land. It shrieked and was lost in a tunnel.

There were only two real things—the cold and the thought of man. The cold expressed itself easily by the whiteness and the leaden shade, the great power of distance, the obliteration of colours, footpaths, landmarks, the silence. Thought was not equally vigorous. It could not sustain itself alone. Men had to walk hard, to talk and even then to change the subjects rapidly, especially if they were abstract. Thus to compare the ham of Wiltshire with that of South Wales was pleasant and easy for a time; but to discuss the nature of love or style or virtue was not long possible.

Under the ice of a pond lay the last summer's nest of a grebe among the rotten reeds. High and low in the hedges, old nests were as the jetsam of summer's wreck—as if a galleon should be represented by a boot on the shore.

Through the land went a dusky river, and in it a black barge with merrily painted prow. It was guided by a brown woman wearing a yellow scarf and she stood boldly up. In the midst of it a man played on a concertina and sang. The barge was light and high in the water; lonely and unnoticed, it threaded the long curves and still the concertina lamented and the tall woman stood boldly up. As it disappeared the dolorous air began to darken and I knew why that barge stood so high and light—because its cargo was merely all the flowers and the birds and the joys and pains of spring, the contentments of summer, the regrets of autumn, of all men and women who lived through the now dying year; and no one claimed them, no one sought them, no one stood on the bank to salute them.

CHAPTER XXIX

A WINTER MORNING

NIGHT was soon to pass into a winter day as I looked out of the window to see what kind of a world it was that had been, since I began to read, shutting me off effectually from everything but my book.

> And but the flitter-winged verse must tell,
> For truth's sake, what woe afterwards befel,
> 'Twould humour many a heart to leave them thus,
> Shut from the busy world of more incredulous.

The words were still fresh in my brain.

But, outside, the trees and barns and shed were quiet and dim, and as much submerged and hidden from the air in which I had been living as the green streets of motionless lily and weed at the bottom of some lonely pool where carp and tench go slowly. The road went straight away from the window to the invisible beyond; hard and dry, it was trying to shine, as if it recalled the sunlight. Half-way along, at one side, under a broad oak, there was a formless but pregnant shadow. The farm-buildings that lay about the road were huddled, dark, colourless, and indistinguishable because of their shadows; they might have been heaped up by a great plough, of which the road was the shining furrow; they were not so much the vague wreckage of what I had known yesterday, as a chaos out of which, perhaps, something was to be born. Yet the outside world was vaster than it had seemed when I could see three ranges of hills and guess at the sea beyond; and strange it was when the words—

> She saw the young Corinthian Lycius
> Charioting foremost in the envious race
> Like a young love, with calm, uneager face,
> And fell into a swooning love of him—

came back to me. How frail and perilous and small was the poet's shielded world! The outside world threatened it as the smooth escarpment of tall, toppling water threatens the little piping sea-bird. And yet this poet's world was for the time being my life. Beyond his words there were, perhaps, the gay, the dear, the beautiful persons whom I knew; Nobby, the tinker, and many more; but probably they slept; they were vain if they were not fictitious; if they could be supposed to live, my only proof of it was that somehow they were connected with a very distant light that refused to go out among the westward copses. They were hardly more credible than the words of a stale preacher talking of charity, or an artful poet writing of love.

So I clung to Keats, the reality, until the road grew almost white, and under that broad oak some rational, nay, beautiful outlines began to appear, which the shadow enveloped like a cocoon. The outlines were hardly built until they were seen to be a wagon, and its birth out of the shadow was a mighty thing that shared the idiom of stately trees and the motions of great waters and of cliffs that look on sunset and a noble sea. Dimly, uncertainly, powerfully, never quite expressing itself in any known language—

as was natural in what seemed to belong to an early
brood of the giant earth—the wagon emerged, with
ponderous wheels and slender, curving timbers and
trailing shafts. The chariot of Dis coming up to
Persephone looked thus majestic. Yet the wagon
suggested nothing definite, at least no history. It had
no such articulate power. But antiquity played about
it as, an hour before, it had played about my shelves
and books. It was simply the richer for its long life,
like a violin or a wise man; and, like them, it neither
carried its legend on its exterior nor encouraged anything more than joyful surmise.

It was the one cleary visible piece of man's work
among all those potent shadows and uncertain forms
of roof and wall; it was crowned by the last stars.
Becoming clearer as morning came, it was an important
part of the re-creation of the world, and involved in it,
just as a brazen image may seem to be part of the
good fortune or calamity which follows prayer to it.
It filled the white road with emotion. It was more
intelligible than some men are when they say "I
worship" or "I love." Keats left my mind. From
my memory, I added melodies of voice and harp and
reed, and noise of seas and winds in forests and houses
by night, and organ music, with its many demons
blithe and terrible, exploring the skyey roof of some
cathedral and knocking at the clerestory to get out,
floating, sad or happy, about the aisles, and settling
at last to make the old purples and greens and blues
in the glass more solemn than before; and yet I could
not reproduce the melody or anything like it, with
which the old wagon pervaded the farmyard. Slowly
the light came, and the world was filled with it as
imperceptibly as the brain with a great thought. It

fell upon the spokes of the wagon wheel, and they seemed to move. Then all was over.

The clear face of things which it is so hard to enjoy was back again. The determined starlings flew swift and straight overhead. The clouds about the risen sun went stately upon their errands through the sky.

PART III

THE UPLAND

CHAPTER XXX

In front, a tall beechen hill closes up the gulf that runs out of the valley into the heart of the chalk down. The hill fills nearly half the sky, and just above it stands the white full moon, as one who looks over his lands. It warms the low, pale, curdled sky, but does not disturb the darkness of the beeches. All its light seems to fall and settle, as if it would dwell there for ever in the cherry trees on either hand. All are blossoming, and in their branches the nightingales sing out of the blossom, dispersing what ruins remain of the world of yesterday, and building rapidly those tall watch towers that last until dawn, which men may climb and from their summits see what may make them out. of love with the earth.

The past day is long past, the day of fighting, digging, buying, selling, writing; and if there are still men on the earth they are all equal in the trances of passion or sleep; the day to come is not to be thought of. The moon reigns; you rule. The centuries are gathered up in your hand. You and the moonlight and the nightingale and the cherry blossom have your own way with them all night long. It is true then that Virgil, Catullus, Crashaw, Burton, Shelley . . . live still, and Horace, Racine, Bishop Beveridge . . . never lived. You exult because you are alive and your spirit possesses this broad, domed earth. Poor thing as you are, you have somehow gained a power of expression like the nightingale's, a pure translucency like the petals of the flowers; and as never before to man or woman you open your eyes widely and frankly, even the limbs move with the carelessness of the animals, the features lose the rigidity that comes of compromise and suppression.

Walking slowly thus, with a bowed head, you find an image of yourself and the universe in a shallow pool among the trees. The pool is your own mind. The flowers at its edge—hyacinth, primrose, marsh marigold, and all the trees and their foliage—are the intimate and permanent companions of your life, and they are clearly mirrored in the water. An oak draws a long, snaky shadow from side to side, with the head and neck of a sitting dove among the leaves. And there, too, are the stars and the moon, brought down into that homely company of trees and flowers by the shining water, and preserved there in strangely woven patterns; just as in your mind you mingle visions of the world, the past, the imaginary, with your own domestic surroundings and acts, and a changing mood, like a puff of wind across the pool, erases them. How sovereign and proud your own form plunged among these mirrored stars and leaves! On such a night an uncourageous lover, who sat at the edge with his mistress, was lured to a strange boldness by long gazing at the two blissful figures down there among the clouds. "See how fair they are," he said, "and how happy and close. Let us make them kiss." And the shadows kissed in the bosom of the pool.

CHAPTER XXXI

THE FOX HUNT

WE had driven ten miles through a country that rose and fell with large, stormy lines of hillock and hill. A March sun was bright, but a sharpness lingered in the air from last night's frost, like a cold spring in a warm lake. Over the hazy, genial oak woods on the hills sailed slow white gulls all crying "wheel whill" with a shrillness that suited the high blue sky. Sowers went across the long red fields, casting dark seeds that flew in curved clouds before them at each second step and vanished in the wind. On the steep roads the dust whirled in curves as of perfect dancers, which the kestrel repeated on a grand scale high overhead. Thrushes sang at ash tops and in hedges. And we four talked, making such harmonious music to a fine day as men may, with jest and recollection and anticipation of the meet of fox hounds to which we were going, two to ride and two to follow afoot.

Within a mile of the meet we got down at a farmhouse where the horses were awaiting their owners and the yeoman was to join us.

The farm-buildings made almost a complete quadrangle with the side of the house—stables, cow stalls, a granary of ancient stone, a barn with a low-arched Tudor doorway like a broad back ready to receive a weight, and ladders and lengths of oak leaning against the walls. There stood the horses, nodding by their grooms, with restless fetlocks; a red calf flung up its heels amongst the flying, yellow straw; the fowls were stately and fluttered by turns. The house was all white, except for the roof of stone "slats" and the large dark windows. Close to it, away from the farm-buildings, lay the crooked orchard. We passed through the shubbery, without offending its warbling blackbirds, and across a lawn to the door.

The yeoman was of a noble, antique type; of medium height; straight, but mobile, and stooping gently as he listened, with moderate, neat, large-featured head; reticent, slow but beautiful of speech, ready with laughter. He made me think of the last Roman who spoke the speech of Virgil and Cæsar quite pure. He was in his prime, past thirty, the last of his family, and still holding their few hundred acres, a bachelor who had not long since won his captivity from the pale, fair-haired beauty at his side, to judge by her commanding smiles from time to time.

They were sure of a fox, he said; not so sure to kill, because the ground was dry again in spite of last night's frost, and scent bad.

As we stood round the room eating sandwiches—there was yet half an hour before the meet—one asked him if he knew anything of an old house in a valley some miles away. All the doors and walls were panelled with mirrors amidst their bright oak, and as you sat there you saw your party repeated as if through the walls in the neighbouring rooms. He had not time to answer when an old bent and pallid man, his uncle, who had sat unobserved, began to speak in a feeble, singing voice, strangely laughing at times.

"I know the house with the mirrors. The Mere-diths lived there for three hundred years, and I knew the last of them well. She was Arabella. She had no brothers, and there is no child. I was a young man then, and though you may not easily believe it, when you see this arm, I was a fine, strong man. Ha! ha! ha!"

He stopped to chuckle abstractedly, with ambiguous irony at the contrast between his early lustihood and the decrepitude which had coffined it. Perhaps his nephew winced at the garrulity and such irony as the thick laughter disclosed to him, but he did nothing to divert the talk, nor did Enid, his betrothed, when she filled a glass with whisky and water for the old man, who did but admire it with a sudden satisfaction, and then continued:

"Well, I was about the age of my nephew yonder, and I had never known what pain or misery was, except when I was nearly beaten by a gipsy in running down Mowland Hill. I farmed and I hunted, and it was understood that I was to marry an amiable and pretty young woman whom my father admired so much that he was willing that nobody should be my wife if not she. But I was in no haste, and indeed I was not fond of women. Others I knew seemed stupid or frivolous. This one was chiefly busy with the church and the poor. I respected her, and I believe now that she would have looked after me well in my old age. She understood me; we had known one another since we were children, and I used to delight to stop my horse to speak to her on a fine day when I was feeling fresh and gay. At last it was agreed that we were soon to be married, and I did not know why to draw back."

Enid glanced quickly at my host, all the command having left her meek smile, and as quickly dropped her eyes. It seemed to me that the glance betrayed a slender fear or anticipation which she was ashamed of immediately. By this over-rigid tranquillity it may be that her lover gave a similar sign, the only one, and lost on her.

"No,"—the old man paused, as though he would still have liked to unearth some excuse which he might, fifty years back, have made for breaking his troth. "No," he said, questioningly, "I did not know why to draw back. But one day a woman I had sometimes heard of—she had been away at school and with friends almost continually—came over and joined our hunt for the first time—Arabella Meredith. She was over one bank before me, and I thought that Edith would never have done that. We had a good day and a long one. As I was riding back I was pretty well satisfied when with great clatter Miss Meredith rode up to me. She had had a long day and she was hot with her gallop, and yet as she came alongside, I turning my horse so that both curvetted together in the narrow road, she was as fresh as if it had been raining and she just out to take the air, as fresh as a young lime leaf and as clean and, if you understand me, as inhuman in a way, at least I thought so that evening when I was alone. When I saw her eyes, as I soon did, they seemed to belong to somebody else hiding there, and not the woman I had seen jumping.

"'Mr. Arnold,' she said, 'I hear you are to be married . . .'

"'Yes,' I said.

"'Then you will marry me,' she said.

"In a mazy way I said that I would think about it, and she replied instantly:

"'Please ride as far as our house with me—not

but that I can look after myself, though it is fifteen miles away, and the roads bad and dark—and you will have plenty of time to think about it.'

I rode home with her, and I did not think at all, and I did not speak; nor did she, except to the horse; and at the end I said that I would marry her if she were willing.

"'I will think about it,' she said, good night,' and I turned my horse to do the ten miles that divided the house with the mirrors from this. It was an extraordinary thing to do, I think. The next day I told Edith that I could not marry her because I wanted to marry Miss Meredith. There was trouble, but it is a long time ago. Edith never married, but continued to help the church and the poor in another part of the country. She was a good woman."

Enid had flushed—was it angrily?—at the first mention of Arabella. She was become serious and very still, and looked no more at her neighbour who was apparently studying some drawings of spaniels. Seeing the gentle girl's pain I was sorry that I had not helped her in the attempt to check the old man. But that was impossible now.

"Arabella was wonderful," he exclaimed, his old voice slowing to a stronger tone and a new solemnity. "Arabella was wonderful. I believed then that for a man to live as I had lived for so long, and then to see her all suddenly, was the best thing in the world. I used to look at her, and even when I did not see her face, but only her neck and hair and dress and feet, it was just like—like it used to be looking up on a day like this at the blossoming tops of tall elms right in the sky, and hearing the cuckoo's mate up there.

"Twice a week I used to walk over to her house or to some place near by to see her. I don't know which was best—the fine weather or the wet—when I went, for in the rain I used to shut out the noise of the rain with my singing all kinds of songs, and sometimes I used to run and whoop as if the hounds had just killed a fox. It was a long way to walk, and sometimes, especially at night, I used to go almost mad with thinking of all the dense space and time and other people, intervening between her and me. Yet I always refused to ride if a farmer stopped his cart, and took footpaths to avoid them. The train to London which I saw all bright on winter evenings used to give me an odd joy and envy—thinking of all those unknown people as if they were hurrying faster than I to see their sweethearts. I did think her beautiful. When I saw Edith in those days, it was somehow painful, like seeing a lamb lying aside dead in a ditch."

Enid had turned her face away to the window and the lawn. Just so pitiful might she seem were she passed over by her lover.

"I am not going to tell you," the old lover went on, looking at nothing visible, "what we did when we met. I think sometimes now that we were not wise. But we used to walk and walk, and she would tell me about girls and the ways of girls, and her childhood, so that I wished I had been a boy with her. She would praise me and say that if ever anything happened to me so that I was hurt and maimed, or if I should die, she would not go on living. The thought of such a thing made her angry and she would stop, and, without looking at me and seeming to forget me, would lift her arms and say confused things that sounded fierce which I could not hear, and then suddenly turn to me quite happy again.

"It was the finest day in my life, when, one May day, we fished together, and cooked some fresh-caught trout by the riverside over a fire of oak branches, and ate them together in the morning, just as the sun grew hot.

"Every day I wished to marry her, especially when she spoke suddenly after being silent, or when I could only smell her lovely breath and see the pale skin under her little ear in the dark.

"She did extraordinary things and she made me do extraordinary things.

"One day as we were walking we heard the sound of the Fair, and Arabella said that we must go. As quick as thought she knocked some walnuts off a tree and we stained our faces with the juice of the rind, and at a friendly cottage borrowed a rude disguise, for we went as gipsies. Arabella told fortunes, first, and I had to tell some too. Then she wanted me to play on a flute while she danced; but instead I kept somewhere near while she danced, to see that all was as it should be; and as it was, I nearly had to knock down a little Welshman whose harp she began dancing to; for while he played and she danced I hardly knew what was happening; it was as if I had gone into a church with rich windows out of a dark night. She danced all the way home, sometimes with her right hand just touching my right shoulder and looking up at me—Ah! Perhaps she thought I was a little careless at seeing her as much in love with me as I with her, and suddenly taking her hand off my shoulder she said quite fiercely that I must do something to show that I would do anything for her."

Here the old man stopped and laughed and drank his whisky and seemed disinclined to go on. The yeoman rose hastily and we had to follow at once, all but Enid, the old man, and the boldest and worst horseman who was taking some more "jumping powder" with an air; and then, when all had mounted in the farmyard, I found courage to equal my curiosity and asked the yeoman for the end of the story. He stopped his impatient horse and said:

"One night in November, when the river was in flood, my uncle remembered what Miss Meredith had said, and in his clothes he swam over instead of going round by the bridge. It was a long and difficult swim and he got bruised on the rocks; but he got through and then went to meet Miss Meredith. I do not know what happened that evening, but the next day his life was in danger from fever, and for many days he was ill. As soon as she heard, Miss Meredith came over and saw him when he was at his worst; I think someone told her that he would recover, being so vigorous a man. Some days later they picked her out of the river, and they say she had drowned herself. My uncle says that as he lay ill he was proud, and did not even ask for Miss Meredith lest she should see him as he was. But when he got downstairs and felt well and was growing stronger, they told him that she was buried in Mowland churchyard. Then he laughed terribly with long laughs, so that they say my grandmother heard him in London, and went on laughing at the magnificent jest of that beautiful woman being underground.

"She was small, with fair skin and brown hair that was pure gold where it was rolled up behind her ear, and she had a deep clear voice. Her skill in dancing was great, and as a rider only my uncle excelled her. She was generous and tender, but courageous and unforgiving, never losing either friend or enemy.

"He has quite recovered now. It is wonderful what things a man will recover from. He does not mind telling the story; I think he is even a little ashamed of his infatuation. All the women who were born in that house, at least all the Merediths, are said to have been odd, and they were all beautiful."

"It is well for all of us," said one, "that there are not many Arabellas in the world."

"There are not many," said the yeoman; and he was about to follow the rest when I saw Enid, a little anxious and it may have been apologetic, at the door. "Good-bye, Arabella," he called, with quiet raillery.

"No!" she stamped her foot impatiently, but gently even so. He kissed her hand and looked at her; and as he rode away, I saw that she was at peace again. He shouted that they would see us by the gorse.

And so those three rode away and we walked to the meet. All the labourers on the farm where the hounds met had a holiday, and all the children too, enough of them to drown the music of the hounds. There were about twenty men and women riding, three in pink, two or three rich men and as many rich women, a lawyer, a doctor, and many farmers and their boys; and every one talked with every one. They found a fox in the long, tumbling hill of gorse that ran almost to the river's edge; but the scent was bad, and after running backwards and forwards for some time, they drew several little covers and there were some rapid bursts with merry music, and flying of dust on the ploughland and halloos here and there, and laughter and chatter of boys, and slow comment from the labourers. But soon all was quiet, except that a child was telling a blind farmer where the hounds were and which way they were going.

The river ran at our feet in one large curve, and among banks not so steep but that it shone continually. Just below us the lover must have swum, landing in the tall oaks that came to the edge. On the farther side a road went up from the low bridge and over the hill, and then, but out of sight, down to the house with the mirrors. Ten miles away, above the river, with its church tower against the sky in a manner that commanded every one who could walk, was the little town where they still hold a Michaelmas Fair. Beyond that, faint and delicate, small and beautiful as the lines in an oyster shell, were great hills all but invisible in haze.

CHAPTER XXXII

APPLE BLOSSOM

THE stream going helpless and fast between high banks is gloomy until it is turned to bright, airy foam and hanging crystal by the mill; over the restless pool below hangs a hawthorn all white and fragrant and murmurous with bloom.

Above the mill, to the north, the land rises in long, lustrous, melodiously swelling lawns of perfect green to the dark borders of a beech wood, where the sweet, thick air fills the hollows among the virginal foliage with blue. In one place the beeches have parted and made a broad avenue for the eye to travel towards a noble stone house, many-angled, many-windowed, grey, discreet, holding, or on such a day seeming to hold, human life worthy to walk upon the long lawns to the mill, where now nothing moves except the divine sunlight and, in the hollows, its little cloudy elves.

Below the mill, to the south, is a land of tall trees standing in conclaves of woods, in whispering groups, or solitary, each in its sovereignty of shade and shining grass; of apple orchards and farmhouses that lie, amidst their haystacks and ricks of straw, in gulfs among the trees; and here and there the yellow skeleton of an oak, encircled by its bark and twigs in piles, thrusts its sharp appealing lines through the neighbouring green.

There is the tall, stony beech, its bole as fair as

human shoulders and flanks, lighted and shadowed' changefully, its topmost branches curving over as if with the weight of birds alighting, and doves and wood wrens among the leaves; the twisted birch's misty, moving foliage as of a pensive fountain; the oak, whose dark branches only yesterday were inter-woven like the flight of many bats at twilight, now an enchanted hill of glowing bronze; the straight, lean, athletic ash, like a young prince in short hunting tunic; the calm, feminine sycamore whose fresh foliage hangs in folds as of smoke; the pollard willow, along the stream, an ancient, neglected, grotesque deity, reluctantly assuming its green garlands for yet another spring.

These things and many more the eye sees delightedly, and having ranged, finds its chief joy in some narrow tract of the large land, like the first field below the mill.

It is but an acre or two of sweet, undulating pasture, bounded on two sides by tall hawthorn hedges, on the third by an ash copse, on the other by an orchard of apple trees. The grass is pure green, revealing here and there a purple orchis or dog violet or blue self-heal, except where the crystal brook rushes through it and gathers white and gold about its banks. Here no shadow falls, or if it does the dew and blossoms break it up. The leaning and interwoven apple trees make a white and wine-filled sky by their dense clots of bloom. The swallows embroider the air with their songs and their blue flight. A farmhouse walls are dusky red between the trunks. Overhead, the dim blue sky lets a white cloud roll out at intervals like lilies from a pool. And the blackbird perfects his song indolently; the thrush thinks clearly, sharply aloud, with nothing long drawn out; and the willow wren happily complains for ever—a voice that has wings and must revolve continually through the land to express for one or another the vague pains or pleasures of a spring day.

The hedges and the orchard and the copse shut out everything except that, through the ash stems, there is the dim, white sea far off, gentle, like a fantastic tale of men and women that never were, in countries where no discoverer's keel has ever shrieked upon the beach, to which the eye wanders now and then, returning again to the apple blossom and the grass with an added security.

Over the green grass walks the farmer's daughter in a white dress, on her head a mushroom-shaped straw hat that reveals black hair curving like the wings of a dove over the half-moon of her brow, and like smoke above her golden nape. She stands still like a straight birch in heavy snow—her form and her dress one and yet separate, and definitely female in rise and fall. She walks like a summer cloud, except that her feet, clad in shining black, take firm hold upon the grass and spurn it strongly, yet with the light short steps of a proud bird. Her left hand carries purple orchis and white stitchwort, and carefully, but fantastically and unnecessarily, raises the hem of her skirt to the height of the tallest dandelions. Her right hand is free to gather flowers, to feel the growth of the young greenfinches in the nest, to arrange and disarrange her hair. Her small round head is lifted up, her eyes fully round, her lips too much curved to meet very often yet, her nose clear and straight, and the fair, wing-like curve of bone from ear to chin seeming to be born of the shadow which it creates upon her neck. Her childhood has passed, her maturity has not come.

She is a Lady May, careless, proud, at ease. On her lips, indeed, is a childish song; but she has become more strange and distant to children than older women are, for the moment—perhaps for to-day only, since to-morrow she may meet a man and stay late in the lanes. She is as strange as the silver water that gushes among green grass and marigold in the copse, or as the blue swallow slanting down the sunny red wall. To look at her is to take deep breaths as at the savour of warm bread, of honeysuckle, of cows when they come from the meadows into a dusty road. A speech that should be all sapphires and pearls would not be worthy of her—to-day. She is at the altar of Aphrodite "full of pity"—to-day. She has been carried far in the goddess's dove-drawn chariot over mountains and seas, and has bathed in the same fountain as Aphrodite, nor yet been seen of men—to-day. Delay, sun, above the sea; wait, moon, below the hills; sing, birds; rustle, new-leaved beeches; for to-morrow and the day after and for ever until the end this will be but a memory and may be all she has. She walks hardly faster than the shadows over the fair grass; and you, Time, O Woodman! set not your axe at the foot of this tree, lean not upon it with your strong hands. See! the crest nods and the air trembles; let it not fall to-day.

CHAPTER XXXIII

A LITTLE BEFORE HARVEST

SUMMER is perfect now.

The wheat says so, when in the dawn it drips with half an hour's rain and gleams like copper under the fresh, dim sky; it cries aloud the same when it crackles in the midday sun, and the golden sea of it washes murmurously to the feet of the hills.

In the hedges and fields the agrimony wands and mullein staves, the climbing vetch, the cushioned bird's-foot lotus, the myriads of ragwort and sow-thistle, are golden too.

The meadowsweet and honeysuckle flowers and the wild carrot seeds give out sweet scents, but not so strong as not to be drowned, when the wind blows, by a thousand lesser scents from field and wood and farmyard.

Wood-pigeons coo in the high-shaded stories of the beeches and in the wet willow copses where bushes and herbage have grown so dense that hardly a bird's-nester or a lover would care to penetrate them. In the dark wood alleys, all day long, hang insects whose wings seem to be still in their swiftness, like golden lamps.

The gardens have amber lilies, fuchsia trees, phloxes, poppies, hollyhocks, carnations, snapdragons, rockets, and red flax rising above rose of Sharon and lemon-scentedleno balm and yellow stonecrop, where the tortoise-shell butterflies worship with opening wings.

163

And on the garden walls the purple plums ooze and heave in the sun with yellow wasps that give a touch of horror to the excellent and abounding life of perfect summer.

These things and many more the eye notes carelessly. We are so rich that we do not count our treasure. We record them as contented worshippers their beads. They are but as dust above the corn when the thresher twists his oaken flail. The mother or master of them all seems to be the line of the chalk hills.

The corn sweeps to these hills, and on the strand which divides them is a hamlet of six thatched cottages and a farmhouse, and new haystacks round these, fine and sharp-angled, and old ones carved in steps and supported by props of ash. The cream pans and the churns glitter outside the house. A girl kneels at the brook that flows past and dips a jug among the cresses, trying to catch a trout at the same time. The eye dwells on these for a little while, saying that it could be content there never to wander again, and then rises to the downs, and away it goes, soaring as at the sound of organ or harp. For how proud-thoughted are these long, curving downs, whether they make a highway at noon for round white clouds or at night for the large moon. They uplift and allure and lead far away the eye. The mind follows the eye as the streaming wake follows the ship and is naught without it. Those curves suggest to the mind, confused and languid after long summer days in the lowland, that it also might follow such curves that lead on—surely—to noble thoughts and high discoveries, though without them it will be happy merely in following with joyous undulations to the windy beeches on the farthest height. To see them close by with our last glance before entering an inn is good, or, far off, on a midsummer night when we are to watch the sun rise from the encampment which makes one of them, or to fancy them by the winter fire; but to see them thus, in full summer, when day is separate from day only by brief, perfumed nights of stars, stimulates like a page of saga or history or a perfect rhyme, setting the heart free. "Let us be brave," says a shepherd of these hills.

> In lofty numbers let us rave . . . .
> I 'll borrow Phœbus' fiery jades,
> With which about the world he trades,
> And put them in my plough.
>
> I'll to great Jove, hap good, hap ill,
> Though he with thunder threat to kill,
> And beg of him a boon.
>
> To swerve up one of Cynthia's beams,
> And there to bathe thee in the streams
> Discover'd in the moon. . . .
>
> And to those indraughts I'll thee bring,
> That wondrous and eternal Spring,
> Whence the ocean hath its flowing.
>
> We 'll down to the dark House of Sleep,
> Where snoring Morpheus doth keep,
> And wake the drowsy groom.

And at evening, when the rooks go over, quietly expounding space in the rosy sky, they do not, as in other countries they do, torment the mind; for the ridge of the downs travels the same way and is at the same moment here, just above us, and yonder in the bosom of the sunset, and it gives rest and satisfaction as, but a few hours ago, it gave infinite adventure and happiness therewith.

CHAPTER XXXIV

AUTUMN BELLS

FROM this beechen hill I can see into and across a long pastoral valley at my feet; its gentle sides running east and west are clothed in wood, and at the western end, where the valley leads straight out into the sunset sky, a stone city lies. Beyond this valley to the south are the misty, wooded ridges that hint at other valleys. The sunset light has made the landscape immense, but with the help of autumn it has made it simple too; and the sound of bells in the city seems to have created it, rounded and mellow in outline and hue. The little rounds of hedge-tops and knolls in the meadows and gorse in the higher slopes harmonize and run into the larger rounds of the single oaks in the middle distance, and the still larger rounds of the hills and their cloudy woods, and the clouds above them. A hawk in the air might seem to be carving the outlines of some perfect palm tree as he flies. The white steam also of a slow train far away bubbles up in the moist and gentle air and hangs there long in delicately changing and merging mounds that mock the clouds and woods. The amber wheat stacks are of the same family of form, lying in a half-circle at one side of a hunched farmhouse that lifts up a dome of mossy thatch—near it a garden of shadowed wallflower, snapdragon, roses, in clouds beyond clouds, with a burning edge of hollyhock, sunflower, red-hot poker, and chrysanthemum.

The sound of the city bells continues to overflow in bubbles from the valley, up and up, to the round, golden clouds. As if filled with the sound, the city smoke ascends and takes on the colours of the sunset.

The sun is now low between the final walls of hill, where the valley ends, and it seems to belong to the city below, as if it were the city's god descending there for once in answer to some especially rich altar or noble deed. The towers and their bells are as maidens pensively embroidering, and now and then dropping their embroidery to sing a melody of something far away; and long after the sun has gone and the city has disappeared their song is repeated in the fragrant and noiseless abysses of the far-stretched night.

CHAPTER XXXV

THE morning air of autumn smelt like the musky, wild white rose. The south wind had carried hither all the golden and brown savours from Devon and Wiltshire and Surrey; and the strong sweetness made the walker snuff deeply at it, with uplifted upper lip. Church bells two miles away, deep among the woods that lay around narrow gulfs of meadow on every side, called and called, as if they had wedded this perfume and all the gold and brown of the wide land. Not the last willow wren in the oak, nor the cooing dove, spoke more melodiously of autumn and repose than the bells. So when I came to the church, under a cavernous beech wood, I paused beneath the low tower and sate in the cool nave.

Parts of the windows were still rich with old colour, the rest might seem to have flown into the woods as the sounds from the genial bells were still flying thither and through the autumn land. The church was the lovely home of the dead of several fair families still living near. A helmet with motionless crest jutted over the nave. Several bright, crude effigies flaunted their crimson and blue in one aisle. The walls were still half covered by paintings of varying clearness. Here and there a sword stood out quite clear, or the head of a woman or a youth, a coat of armour, an aureole that some head had lost, a curve of vesture, or a mere whisper of colour, red like old blood, or

168

a few words, such as "olim magnificus pulcherrimus" — "periit" — "resurget"; things that survived there much as events in human memories, and as incidents and expressions may actually survive our death, and painfully strive for integration in a dim world of fragments that shall be strangely arrayed again.

The clerk stood looking out of a little open window that revealed a piece of green meadow and yellow maple that might have belonged to the ancient glass.

One by one the men came in, two old labourers past work, a neighbouring farmer, his cowman and carter, a gamekeeper, and the women and children in twos and threes, and lastly the squire — perhaps twenty-five altogether. In hymn and psalm and prayer all voices save those of the rector and one sweet-voiced child were so faint that the church was undisturbed. The old men were still, the young restless, the women and children interested in one another; but they were fainter than the figures on the wall, being so like thousands of others, all but a red and fair-haired man of fifty who might have been a Bacchus hastily meta-morphosed for some jolly purpose.

With the sermon the silence became immense, as if it must flower suddenly or crumble away in a roar. The preacher spoke slowly as one who scorned time, and in the intervals could be heard the masticating of horses in the meadow outside. He spoke of the necessity of "drawing near to God" — by a life of piety, by private prayer, by communion, by worship-ping in this house. His rich, gentle voice saying murmurous things fell upon me as one of sleep's forerunners, and I had just heard him asking the squire and the Bacchus and the rest whether they had not, at the Communion, had visions of "those tabernacles above," when I began to dream a dream which the parson could not have inspired without the help of some very different elf who now lay under the pavement of the nave, or was painted on the wall, or had sat among the rushes when the church was beautiful and young as a country bride. For it seemed that I saw these men and women in a kind of heaven where all day long for ever they did those things which had most pleased or most taken hold of them in life. I saw them like the figures painted on the wall, some bright and clear, some dim or broken, some known by hardly more than a defacement of the large light that dwelt there.

There the grave and cheerful carter went home at evening, looking ahead steadily, without sorrow, or alarm, or lassitude, and sometimes turning to his undulating team, noting their still bright harness and speaking to them by name: "Ho! Violet" — "Smiler" — "Darling" — "Swallow." He was even now hungry, a little tired, thinking of his inn at nightfall. Heaven had caught him and made of him a picture of strength, contentment, and evening which, in that luminous land, was pleasing yet to mortal men.

There the cowman was leading out the bull, and making the ring jar in its nostrils. Still his back and knees were bent as he cursed out "Jimmy," his face still moulded and unmoulded by faint-hearted lust, vexation, fear, perplexed by the home where his eleven children were, with his pigs and his fledgeling-magpies.

His wife was near, but almost invisible, and, as it were, a wraith of pitiful maternity, neither bitter nor glad, but bearing her burdens, one still beneath her girdle, one in her arms, and others demanding her anxiety, winning her tenderness, on this side and on that.

The gamekeeper stood, with smoking gun barrels, and a cloud of jay's feathers still in the air and among the May foliage about him. Pride, stupidity, servility clouded his face as in his days of nature, and above him in the oaks innumerable jays laughed because beauty, like folly, was immortal there.

The squire, more faint, and whether to his joy or not I could not discern, was standing under a bough on which hung white owls, wood owls, falcons, crows, magpies, cats, hedgehogs, stoats, weasels, some bloody, some with gaping stomachs, some dismembered or crushed, some fleshless, some heaving like boiling fat, and on them and him the sun shone hot.

The red-faced man sat drinking ale, and with him it seemed always evening, and his stomach fathomless.

Five boys—four of them with blackened faces and sticks or swords, and one of them dressed as a woman and carrying a bag—played the Pace-Egging Play in blue Easter weather in a daffodil lane before a ripe grey farmhouse.

A little girl nursed something musingly, whether a mole or a cluster of rags I could not tell.

The farmer sat on his cream pony, brow-beating a bird-nesting boy by a gate.

A young woman waited by a stile and did up her hair.

And still the parson threw back his head and closed his eyes, and with an action as of washing his hands, talked melodiously and with satisfaction, saying, at last, "It is well for us to draw near unto the Lord."

PART IV

THE MOUNTAINS

CHAPTER XXXVI

It was one of those early March days in a mountainous country when a warmly clothed man, in good health and walking rapidly, can just foretaste the spring. The icy dark waters in stony brooklets shone golden whenever it could find the sun. This gold seemed a brand upon the winter that marked it for death. There was gold also on the turf between the walls and the roadways, for there were hundreds of celandine flowers: it was to be found also in the miniature forests of the moss that made detached and placid worlds upon every stone of the walls; in the little hollow woods, or steep and craggy orchard plots, where the first daffodils were unveiled; in the rick-yards where fowls scattered the gleaming straw; in the fur of the squirrel that moved as if the swirling wind dissolved and shaped it again continually; in the warm ale at "The White Hart."

But when the eye grew proud and the wind rose and every half-hour the horizontal snow put out everything of the world except its noises—the cry of the curlew, the buzz of pewits' wings, the song of the missel thrush that came through the storm like a mere ode to liberty in the midst of revolution—then it was winter still, and the rustling oak leaves talked of December. And when the snowfall ceased with a rush as if upon the wings of a peregrine, those small signs of spring were no more than a child's sand

175

castles on a vast seashore, and not so noticeable as the thick suds and flakes of snow hanging from the hedges on the walls and turned to mists by the restless robins.

On one side, for some miles, ran a large fell that was a home and playground of winds, steep and long to be crossed, and all white and grim, shutting out home and the pleasures that are found among men. On the other side, steep also and wildly shaped with small, precipitous crags and angry surf of heather and here and there haggish thorns, lay a moor. Between these two the road rose and fell over lesser but steep hills, and from one hilltop I could see the sea beyond the moor. It was grey, without light, with long quivering lines that never ended, but insubstantial; it seemed rather the grisly offspring of a mind made pregnant by the wintry melancholy. The mountains came down to the edge of it, like lions to drink, ten miles away. Not a house was visible, and on the sea the few ships were like the water itself, inventions of my own, as it were, which I had launched upon that infinite desolation for sport;

All day, ahead and always at the same distance, rose high mountains, with crude outlines as of heavy and frosty land fresh turned by the plough; the long ravines of snow upon their sides made their peaks more sharp and their heights more sudden. They haunted the day.

Now and then the snow fell, and in the weak sunshine that followed, the light struck up from the snow and made the white breasts of the gulls seem opal lanterns full of flame, and the hazel thickets were nets of silver and crystal branches, invisible in their own splendour.

I descended to a small deep river that ran, with noble curves of power, solemn and full of some in-human simple purpose. For a moment the sunlight fell on one curve of it and the windy waves were now a stately glittering cavalcade, and now a dance of fairies into which some ass-headed Bottom suddenly intruded with a gust from a cloud, making them whirl faster and then disappear. But the river was careless of the light; it went on as before, unchanged even when for another moment all that grim, serious water was changed into white spray and light by a fall.

And there still were the mountains ahead. Their painful distances of long, white, houseless steeps made the mind suffer the body's agony of toiling there, of being lost there in storm, of being there on a still, dark night. They bred—by means of natural, human sym-pathy with the difficulty of life among such heights, by the horror of the distance, the coldness, the white-ness—a languor out of which emerged infinite admira-tion and awe, a sense of beauty even, and unquestion-ably a kind of pride in the powers of the human spirit that can dwell upon the earth and be the equal of these things, sharing with them the sunlight and the darkness, enduring like them vicissitudes, decay, vio-lent disaster, and like them disbelieving in the future and in death, except for others. So when at nightfall the snowy hills made a semicircle round the head of an enormous grey estuary, and couched there ten and fifteen and twenty miles away as if the sweep of a puissant arm had made them in clearing a space for the water, they were purely beautiful, while over them a large, simple sunset threw a golden bridge between towering, white, still clouds.

Then, at length, a hamlet on a hill; first, a farmyard

on one side of the road and a farmhouse on the other; then four or five stone cottages; lastly an inn where I thought to sleep. Hardly had I sat down than a pedlar came in and sat beside me. He was a tall, grave man of a gritty, brown complexion and big, straight features; from his simple, heroic face, that seemed an animated piece of crag from his native hills, his blue eyes looked at me with that glance, fearless of any return, which the ordinary man gives to a dog or a labourer, but presently became more modest as I looked up and down the blue gaberdine which he wore down to his knees.

The gaberdine was of the stoutest linen, heavy and warm. It opened for about six inches down from the neck, back and front, and was fastened with small bone buttons. On each side of these openings it was smocked in an elaborate pattern nine inches deep; the wide, turn-down collar almost covered the embroidered shoulder straps and was itself adorned with seven rows of feather stitching. The sleeves were smocked both at the shoulders and the wrists, and were finished with broad, feather-stitched cuffs. He wore it because it was decent, and he would always wear one so long as the woman lived who could make it.

I asked him about his trade, and he said that he pursued it among these hills and valleys all the winter, setting it aside for work in the fields during the summer months. He was born in one of the cottages close by; so was his father before him and so were his children after him. They were happy there. Death alone disturbed them now and then; and death, he said, was incurable and to be expected. In the spring he spent less on candles and his orchard bloomed, and there was a marriage or two in the church and the ewes dropped their lambs. In the summer it was warm without fires, and they needed no candles, and he had what he desired—what that was he did not say. In the autumn he remembered that things were coming round again, winter soon and then spring again. In the winter his cottage walls were thick, and if the days were short he had always had a fire and some food, and had never yet refused a beggar something; there were songs also; and as to his trade, of course he liked it, and he did not think people could do without him.

"And now, young man," he said, "who are you, what have you seen, and what is your country?"

He looked at me with something like the benignity of a child accepting a spoonful of honey; but for that joy and expectancy I might have spoken easily. I hesitated between the truth, which was difficult and perhaps to him unintelligible, my own view of the truth, which would be so confused by reservations and afterthoughts that it could not please, and the picturesque. So I said:

"I am a poor, modern man"—which was true—"I have seen nothing"—which was my view of the truth—and finally, "the great city of London is my country"—which was picturesque.

"What?" said he, not angrily, nor pityingly, but inquiringly, "what do you mean by a 'poor, modern man,' and how is it that you have seen nothing?"

A thousand things crowded to my brain and contended on my lips. This was an opportunity, but too great a one, too sudden. I stifled my designs and decided to say nothing. He was kind; he nodded gracefully and continued:

"Tell me about London."

He did not say, "Do me an essay of fifteen hundred

words by next week." That might have been easy: writing—possibly even good writing—is comparatively easy; because the writer is alone while he writes and is not present while his work is read, and he can therefore withhold what seems difficult to express and he deceives without appearing deceitful; moreover, he writes at his ease, or should do, what is probably read in haste. But in conversation with an aged blue-eyed man, in a majestic blue gaberdine, who has an evening's leisure and desires the truth, asking simply, "Tell me about London," the difficulties in the way of a simple man are enormous. I said something about a book called *The Soul of London*; but he could not read. He wished again to be informed what the soul of a city was. Again I failed him.

"But you have actually lived in London," he repeated, encouraging me.

"Yes." He seemed to be proud, as who should say, "I sit with one who has lived in the most famous city in the world."

I remembered that there are said to be five millions of human beings in London, and that its streets on end would reach to the moon.

Also I thought of the old song and the verse:

> There be kings and queens in London town
> A-sitting all of a row.

In despair I actually ventured to tell him that there were five million people there. But he seemed to be poor at arithmetic and he was frank.

"I beg you," he said, "to speak simply and not all at once to a poor, remote old man. The evening is young yet," he continued without heat and as if he were making all clear.

"There is a king there, is there not?" he said.
"There is."
"And a queen?"
"Yes."
"And a palace?"
"There are several palaces."
"Then tell me about the king," he said.

I have never seen the king, and I longed for the power of the Tempter to tell the old man of:

> Prætors, proconsuls to their provinces
> Hasting, or on return, in robes of state;
> Lictors and rods, the ensigns of their power;
> Legions and cohorts, turms of horse and wings;
> Or embassies from regions far remote,
> In various habits, on the Appian road,
> Or on the Æmilian —

But still his questions came. How did the ships come up and unlade again? What were the army and the navy like? Had I seen the famous men? Were the people noble as became a metropolitan race? Achilles questioning Ulysses in Hades could not have spoken more magnificently than this old man questioning me, though I seemed the ghost and he the visitor to the underworld. Yet in some sort his great questions, elevating his soul, seemed to supply him, if not with an answer, at least with some satisfaction. I would have spoken, if I could. But how short the evening! myself how unprepared and inadequate! I would have told him of Pimlico and Battersea which were not entirely unknown to me. I would have said that there were sorrowful and happy men there—thousands of both, unknown to me and unknown to one another; thousands of houses, beautiful, stately, pompous, indifferent, ugly, sublimely squalid; that upon them

as upon him and his neighbours fell rain and sun
and snow and the wind beat and death came suddenly,
desired or undesired; that the city was as vast as
Time, which had made it, and that to know it a
man must live and die the lives and deaths of all
that had ever lived and died there. But he ceased
to regard me. He entered into talk with others that
came in. One sang this ballad and he, like the rest,
joined the chorus:

My clothing was once of the linsey woolsey fine,
My tail it grew at length, my coat likewise did shine;
But now I'm growing old, my beauty does decay,
My master frowns upon me; one day I heard him say —
        Poor old horse, poor old horse.

Once I was kept in the stable snug and warm,
To keep my tender limbs from any cold or harm;
But now, in open fields, I am forced for to go,
In all sorts of weather, let it be hail, rain, freeze, or snow,
        Poor old horse, poor old horse.

Once I was fed on the very best corn and hay
That ever grew in yon fields, or in yon meadows gay;
But now there's no such doing can I find at all;
I'm glad to pick the green sprouts that grow behind yon wall.
        Poor old horse, poor old horse.

You are old, you are cold, you are deaf, dull, dumb, and slow,
You are not fit for anything or in any team to draw;
You have eaten all my hay, you have spoilèd all my straw;
So hang him, whip him, stick him, to the huntsman let him go.
        Poor old horse, poor old horse.

My hide unto the tanners, then I would freely give
My body to the hound dogs, I would rather die than live;
Likewise my poor old bones that have carried you many a mile
Over hedges, ditches, gates and bridges, likewise gates and stiles.
        Poor old horse, poor old horse.

Terrible, noble old man! No doubt he expected me to speak as simply as that, so I slipped away from him and went to the next inn. A high, cloudy night hung over me, like a great yew tree in March, with stars instead of flowers. With those reticent, dark silences and spaces I tried to console myself.

CHAPTER XXXVII

THE MIRROR

THERE are a hundred little landscapes on the walls by the roadside—of grey or silver or golden stone, embossed and fretted and chequered by green and gold-pointed mosses, frosty lichens, pale round pennywort leaves, and the orange foliage of cranesbill. At their feet are the young leaves of the larger celandine and the lustrous blossoms of the lesser, still swaddled in dead leaves where mice and squirrels are questing. On top, thorns and ash trees trail horizontally in many dragon shapes, and purple brambles overhang. Or there are low thorns which make way at intervals for straight hollies, spared by the billhook, or even carved by it into pagoda-like shapes. Sometimes even a thorn has been thus spared and honoured, but here they are not each knotted into impenetrable globes of twigs or interlaced in pairs as elsewhere. What fantasy persuades men to make those little wayside and even railwayside suggestions of a mild tree worship surviving yet? In places the walls are interrupted and replaced by a smooth, blue sheet of natural rock based in grass and making a home for vertebrate ferns, and stamped by white and yellow and green algæ which look as if they were the stains of a sunshine too strong to be wiped out. Some of the ash-tree boles are heavily draped in a fur woven inextricably of dark green and fine-leaved ivy, pale green moss over which hover pendulous drops of gold, silver lichen, and ferns green and amber. Out of rock or wall gushes bright, crystal water, losing itself in moss and herbage below, or received into small stone tanks, and turned into a darkly gleaming, golden creature that throbs under the rain.

Between such walls the road winds into many valleys and over many fells towards the mountains. On either hand rise and fall many hollowed tawny meadows, with boulders embedded in heather and flowering gorse, and over them the pewits plunge and soar and modulate their crying by their speed. Here and there a family of oak or beech stands up in the midst of the fields. Between the meadows there are copses of hazel and oak, and snowdrops underneath, or a crisp, un-trodden carpet of old leaves of many dying golds and browns and reds; or an arable field intervenes. The plough climbs the hill, turning the dry, grey soil to purple and brown that is dappled by rooks and gulls. Some of the gulls slide overhead against the wind, inclining their wings this way and that, rising and descending slightly, as if they could, by tacking and delaying, avoid the streamy wind.

The steeper hills are the home of oak and ash and birch and larch. The grey larch woods waver in colour like a dying trout, as the wind and the sunshine pass over them. In a five-minute shower the rainbow sets her foot among the trees before she leaps across the sky, and while yet her colours are uncertain among the luminous branches makes a small, fairy, remote world that speaks to the eye like the young moon on a fair evening, or Cassiopeia when it crowns a sapphire night.

In ten miles there is an inn. "Pretty Polly" and

"Sceptre" are on the walls, with notices of sales and advertisements of spirits. The hostess sings the cosmic melody of "Blue Bell" as she goes about her work—that marvellous melody over which farm boys become romantic and even cheerful at four o'clock on wild and sleety mornings in January as they go about their work. But the host has good ale, and he can sing the Holm Bank Hunting Song:

One morning last winter to Holm Bank there came
A noble, brave sportsman, Squire Sands was his name,
Came a-hunting the fox, bold Reynard must die,
And he flung out his train and began for to cry,
    Tally-ho, tally-ho! Hark forward, away, tally-ho!

The season being frosty, and the morning being clear,
A great many gentlemen appoint to meet there;
To meet with Squire Sands with honour and fame
And his dogs in their glory to honour his name.

There Gaby the huntsman with his horn in his hand,
It sounded so clear and the dogs at command,
Tantive! Tantive! the horn it did sound,
Which alarmed the country for above a mile round.

It's hark dogs together, while Jona comes in,
There's Joyful and Frolic, likewise little Trim,
It's hark unto Dinah, the bitch that runs fleet,
There's neat little Justice, she'll set 'em to reet.

There's Driver and Gamester, two excellent hounds,
They'll find out bold Reynard if he lies above ground;
Draw down to yon cover that lies to the south,
Bold Reynard lies there, Trowler doubles his mouth.

Three times round low Furness they chased him full hard,
At last he sneaked off and through Urswick churchyard,
He listened to the singers as I've heard them say,
But the rest of the service he could not well stay.

The dogs coining up made Reynard look sly,
Then he marked out his tricks for to give'em the by;
They being bred to their business they managed their cause
And they made him submit to their attention close.

Through Kirkby and Woodland they nimbly passed,
Broughton and Dunnerdale they came to at last,
Then down across Duddon to Cumberland side,
And at Grass-gards in Ulpha, bold Reynard he died.

Since Reynard is dead he'll do no more ill,
He hadn't much time for to make a long will,
He has left all his states to his survivor and heir,
He has a right to a widow for she'll claim her share.

Of such a fox chase as never was known,
The horsemen and footmen were instantly thrown,
To keep within sound didn't lie in their powers,
For the dogs chased the fox eighty miles in five hours.

You gentlemen and sportsmen wherever you be,
All you that love hunting draw near unto me,
Since Reynard is dead, we have heard of his downfall,
Here's a health to Squire Sands of High Graythwaite Hall.
    Tally-ho, tally-ho! Hark forward, away, tally-ho!

The road has turned away into a valley. The mountains are close ahead, and the billowy moorland prepares me for them, with hawks in all its hollows, and small ponds, the silent sport of winds that roar in crags and hiss in grasses, and then at length a long, blue pool, edged by yellow reeds and receiving the shadow of a steep oak wood. There the wind is lured into many metamorphoses among the ripples—at one moment a writhing, hundred-headed snake, at another the wraith perhaps of a swift skater who was once drowned in the water, and again a swarm of dark bees. At first sight this blue expanse, with narrow ends running into the moorland, and its edge of shivering reed, lays hold upon the mind. All day, unseen of any but the shepherd, the water reflects the birds and the clouds, and all night the stars, until it might be supposed to have acquired a symbolic sadness and tranquillity by thus keeping watch on all the nights and days since it began. There, in its depths, hang the mountain clouds and the immense spaces of sky, with something added by the reflecting water, as if it were some gloomy opiate personality that turned all things to its own tune. Even the joyous, golden fleeces of the perfect summer morning are rendered by the pool with touches of wizardry and night, and when a little breeze erases them for a moment it is like a breath of delight sweeping over an immortal pain. The nearest mountain, too, is there. The highest summit, engraved with snow, shows in the depths like a bleached skull emerging from ridgy tracts of dark sand. There, also, are the long, tawny and olive flanks of the ascent, inlaid with purple and blue by precipices and cloud-shadows, with grey and ruddy woods below, and the silver wounds of birches. Now and then my own shadow flits among them, as if a magician had compelled me to wander in that giddy profound of water and sky. As I look down I seem to see what men have made of the universe in the past, with the help of poet and priest, by plunging it in the sorrows and uncertainties of their own heart and brain. There is superstition, there religion and poetry, confining the great heavens and the hills with sun and moon and stars, within these few acres of desolate mountain water. There are the stories of the gods and of a heaven that overhung mortals with hideous aspect. There, also, the eager courage of man's soul when first he tried to burst "the strong bars of Nature's gateways"—while the sun and wind contend upon the water—and set out upon the adventure which has made us "equal with heaven." Looking up, away from the pool, there still are the mountains and the sky, just as they were, still inscrutably holding out in one hand laughter and in one hand tears for us to choose from. I look down and the singing lark, against a white cloud, is singing high and wise things in some contemplative poet's verse. I look up and, behold I the new joy of the spring, unintelligible, and for the moment not asking to be understood, but to be shared; and as we climb happily the pool no longer imposes its version of life, for yonder is the True upon the hills, and the eyes dilate and the nostrils and the lungs accept the air and the "darling of men and gods . . . mistress of the nature of things" takes her place with us.

CHAPTER XXXVIII

UNDER THE MOOR

It was June, but it had been like March for many miles upon the rough moor until, with the dawn, I came to a lowland where there were mossy fields with clear rain pools among the flowering gorse; and meadows cut into two planes by small, perpendicular cliffs of stone, so that on one the cattle were already feeding in the early light and on the other still lying down; and wheat fields that had islands of stone in their midst; and then at last an immense meadow sloping down towards fresh oak woods and the sea, and rising out of it rounded beechen knolls which, Druid-like, preserved the night under their domes of foliage, though all the grass was flooded by the slow tides of dawn. The white cow-parsley flowers hovered around me on invisible stems and gave out the thick summer flavours of nettles and myriad grasses. And lying down and sleeping in the sun until morning was hot, I awoke and seemed to hear a tale of the south as the air grew mazy with the scent of elder and thyme and the colour of bird's-foot lotus and all the grass, and the sky leaned down upon the earth in milky purples. It was just such a change from the poor land to the rich as is expressed in the ancient tale of Cherry of Zennor told by Hunt in his *Popular Romances of the West of England*.

The girl, Cherry of Zennor, could not contentedly put up with her life at home, because her parents were poor, living on potatoes and fish, and she, though she was pretty and could run like a hare, had never a ribbon for her curls nor a new frock to go to church or to fair in. So she set out to get a servant's place somewhere in the "low countries."

The road was long and she was homesick by the time she had reached a four-went way. There she sat down and cried, but had scarcely recovered when she saw a gentleman coming up to her. He bade her "good morning," and asked her whither she went; and when she said that she was off to look for a servant's place, he told her that he was in search of just such a clean and handsome girl for his own house. So Cherry went off with him, to milk his cow and look after his child; and she was to have good clothes when she got there.

They went down and down for a long way; the road was clouded over by trees and was growing darker and darker, when suddenly the man opened a gate in a wall and told her that there it was that he lived. She had never seen a garden so rich in fruit and flowers and singing birds. Was it enchanted? But no, the man was no fairy; he was too big. Presently his child appeared, a boy with piercing and crafty eyes, and an old hag, called "Aunt Prudence," who prepared a choice supper for the girl; and she ate of it heartily. Cherry slept with the child at the top of the house and was told that, even if she could not sleep, she was to keep her eyes shut up there and not to speak to the boy; at dawn she was to wash him at a spring in the garden and rub his eyes—never her own—with an ointment; then she was to milk the cow and give the boy a bowl of the last milk; she was at all times to avoid curiosity.

All this she did until it came to milking the cow.

But Cherry saw no cow and was calling, "Pruit! Pruit! Pruit!" when out she came from among the trees as if from nowhere. All day, but it was easy work, she scalded milk, made butter, cleaned platters and bowls with water and sand, picked the fruit, weeded the garden. Sometimes the man kissed her for her pains.

A year passed. Aunt Prudence was sent away because she took Cherry into one of the forbidden rooms, where the floor was like glass and it was full of people turned to stone. Sometimes the master went away and left Cherry alone with the child.

The ointment was still a puzzle—but surely it made the child's eyes see many things.' So one day she anointed her own eyes with it. It burned her painfully, and running to the spring to wash it away she learned its power. For there, at the bottom of the water, was a world of little people at play and among them her master; and looking up she saw that the branches of the trees and the flowers and the grass were crowded with the same joyous people. Another day she looked through the keyhole of one of the forbidden rooms and saw her master there, and many ladies too, all singing, and one of these who looked like a queen he kissed. So when, as they were fruit gathering some time afterwards, the master leaned forward to kiss her, she struck him on the face, saying that he might kiss the small people under the water. Next morning very early he called her from her bed, led her by the light of a lantern up the dark lane for a long way, and then disappeared, after telling her that at times she would still be able to see him on the hills; and when she had recovered from her sorrow she went home.

CHAPTER XXXIX

The first steep cornfield under the edge of the red moor lay all rough and warm with stubble in the evening light. The corn sheaves themselves were of a shining gold and leaned together in shocks that made long, low tents and invited the wayfarer to shelter and sleep. We had come over the moor for hours and this field was the beginning of a deep valley that stretched to the sea. Yonder was the sea, ten miles away, with a row of lights running out upon a nose of land far into it. The valley held one village half-way towards the sea and several white farmhouses which sent the smoke of supper to explore the neighbouring ash trees.

A stream running straight from the moor gave us water and we ate our supper leaning against a corn shock. Our pipes soon went out, what with fatigue and deep indulgence in the warmth and the pleasant valley, brimming with summer haze and golden still.

We had been alone when, just as the light was going, two farm boys and a girl came into the field without noticing us. The girl sat at the top of the field and the boys took off their coats and laid them beside her. She arranged their folds and then sat straight up to watch. For down the field ran the boys, striding heavily side by side, each leaping the same shock until they had reached the bottom wall almost at the same time, where they argued and made claims to victory in broken voices. They walked quickly up again to the girl and threw themselves down panting, close to her, arguing together as much as they could without breath.

The girl laughed and said something; then they rose up and raced again, the heavier one this time encouraging himself with groans at each leap over the sheaves, flinging himself over with such ferocity that he tumbled at the end well in front.

"You can jump, no mistake," said the girl to the winner. "But what 's the matter with you?" she asked the other, putting a foxglove between her lips. Both were too much out of breath to speak, but in a few minutes started again. They ran faster than ever; they leapt well over the tops of the shocks, so high as to stumble at each descent. The winner of the last race could only just keep level with the other, and seemed about to collapse at each thundering jump, when his rival, beginning a great leap too early, fell in the middle of the shock and lost the race. They returned, the winner first, and lay sprawling, panting full in the girl's face.

"Well, Luke, you have won, and there's your kiss," she said to the heavier lad.

"And, John, you have been beaten; we did not say what the loser should have, so here 's two for you," she went on, this time taking the flower out of her mouth. "And now, lads, race again!"

This time the race was never in doubt. John took each leap as if he aimed at the harvest moon that rose before him. Luke tripped at several sheaves, and, at the bottom, climbed over the stone wall and disappeared. As to John, he came back and began racing and leaping alone, until the girl, feeling cold or in need of some company, went off and left the proud fellow to the moon and the line of shocks.

CHAPTER XL

THE night was dark and solid rain tumultuously invested the inn. As I stood in a dim passage I could see through the bar into the cloudy parlour, square and white, surrounded by settles, each curving about a round table made of one piece of elm on three legs. A reproduction of "Rent Day" and a coloured picture of a bold Spanish beauty hung on the wall, which, for the rest, was sufficiently adorned by the sharp shadows of men's figures and furniture that mingled grotesquely. All the men but one leaned back upon the settles or forward upon the tables, their hands on their tankards, watching the one who sang a ballad—a ballad known to them so well that they seemed not to listen, but simply to let the melody surge about them and provoke what thoughts it would.

At some time, perhaps many times in his life, every man is likely to meet with a thing in art or nature or human life or books which astonishes and gives him a profound satisfaction, not so much because it is rich or beautiful or strange, as because it is a symbol of a thing which, without the symbol, he could never grasp and enjoy. The German archers making a target of Leonardo's sculptured horse and horseman at Milan; the glory of purple that has flown from a painted church window and settled upon a peasant's shoulders for an hour; the eloquence, as of an epigram rich in anger and woe, of one bare branch that juts out from a proud green wood into the little midnight stars and makes them smaller with its splendid pang; a woodman felling one by one the black and golden oak trees in the spring and slaying their ancient shadows; or, in a discreet and massive crowd, one jet of laughter, so full of joy or defiance or carelessness that it seems to cut through the heavy air like the whistle of a bullet—the world is one flame of these blossoms, could we but see. Music has many of them in her gift. Music, the rebel, the martyr, the victor—music, the romantic cry of matter striving to become spirit—is itself such a symbol, and there is no melody so poor that it will not at some time or another, to our watchful or receptive minds, have its festal hour in which it is crowned or at least crucified, for our solemn delight. "Dolly Gray" I have heard sung all day by poor sluttish women as they gathered peas in the broad, burning fields of July, until it seemed that its terrible, acquiescent melancholy must have found a way to the stars and troubled them.

And of all music, the old ballads and folk songs and their airs are richest in the plain, immortal symbols. The best of them seem to be written in a language that should be universal, if only simplicity were truly simple to mankind. Their alphabet is small; their combinations are as the sunlight or the storm, and their words also are symbols. Seldom have they any direct relation to life as the realist believes it to be. They are poor in such detail as reveals a past age or a country not our own. They are in themselves epitomes of whole generations, of a whole countryside. They are the quintessence of many lives and passions made into a sweet cup for posterity. A myriad hearts and voices have in age after age poured themselves into the few notes and words. Doubtless, the old singers were not content, but we, who know them not, can well see in their old songs a kind of immortality for them in wanderings on the viewless air. The men and women—who hundreds of years ago were eating and drinking and setting their hearts on things—still retain a thin hold on life through the joy of us who hear and sing their songs, or tread their curving footpaths, or note their chisel marks on cathedral stones, or rest upon the undulating churchyard grass. The words, in league with a fair melody, lend themselves to infinite interpretations, according to the listener's heart. What great literature by known authors enables us to interpret thus by virtue of its subtlety, ballads and their music force us to do by their simplicity. The melody and the story or the song move us suddenly and launch us into an unknown. They are not art, they come to us imploring a new lease of life on the sweet earth, and so we come to give them something which the dull eye sees not in the words and notes themselves, out of our own hearts, as we do when we find a black hearthstone among the nettles, or hear the clangour of the joyous wild swan, invisible overhead, in the winter dawn.

In the parlour of the inn the singer stood up and sang of how a girl was walking alone in the meadows of spring when she saw a ship going out to sea and heard her true love crying on board; and he sailed to the wars and much he saw in strange countries, but never came back; and still she walks in the meadows and looks out to sea, though she is old, in the spring. He sang without stirring, without expression, except in so far as light and darkness from his own life emerged enmeshed among the deep notes. He might have been delivering an oracle of solemn but ambiguous things. And so in fact he was. By its simplicity and remoteness from life the song set going the potent logic of fancy which would lead many men to diverse conclusions. It excluded nothing of humanity except what baseness its melody might make impossible. The strangeness and looseness of its framework allowed each man to see himself therein, or some incident or dream in his life, or something possible to a self which he desired to be or imagined himself to be, or perhaps believed himself once to have been. There were no bounds of time or place. It included the love of Ruy Blas, of Marlowe, of Dante, of Catullus, of Kilhwch, of Swift, of Palomides, of Hazlitt, of Villon. . . . And that little inn, in the midst of mountains and immense night, seemed a temple of all souls, where a few faithful ones still burnt candles and remembered the dead.

PART V

THE SEA

CHAPTER XLI

THE white houses on the hill are whiter than ever before in the early light and the south wind from over the sea. The soft, wheat-coloured sand is inscribed far from the water by the black scrawl of the overpast storm. But now the sea is broken by sliding ripples so small that they seem only the last, discontented efforts of the wind to make the surface one perfect floor of glass. The curving, foamy lines waver and swirl and are about to disappear and leave the desired level when others are born unnoticeably. The black hulls of the leaning ships gleam and darken the water, and by their reflections give it an immeasureable depth which contrasts strangely with its lucid tranquillity and the drowned roses of the departing dawn, for in the high blue sky some of the sunrise clouds have lost their way and hang, still rosy, near the zenith, round the transparent moon. The mist over the sea at the horizon is golden.

Sea and shore are at rest, all but one group of men who are welcoming a little ship that comes in upon the tide, fragrant and stately and a little weary, as with folded arms, solemn also as if she were invading, or perhaps bringing mysterious gifts for, the ancient, wintry land.

And now they are hauling in the deeply-laden boat that seems on this fair morning to have brought the spring out of the sea; and that is why they strain

grimly to have her safe on the storm-strewn shore.
She is laden with flowers, with anemones and primroses for the woods, violets for the banks, marigolds
for the brooks and the ungrazed, rushy corners of
long fields, daffodils for the stone walls and the short
turf at the edges of copses, stitchwort for the hedgerows, bittersweet, may for the hawthorns, gold for the
willows, white and rosy blossom for the old orchards
among the hills, mezereon, jonquils, rockets, plume
poppies and snapdragons and roses for the gardens;
and the men heave and groan as if they feared lest
the sea should still rob them of some.

All the leaves are there—the sweet hawthorn green
which the children chew, the dewy, pensile leaves of
hazel and beech and lime, the palmy ash leaves still
misty with purple flower, the oak leaves bronzed or
gilded among their rosy galls, and the streamers of
the willow, and all the grasses and reeds, and the tall
young adder-headed bracken for the moor, and ferns
for the dripping ledges of the waterfall; and the men
heave without resting, lest any should escape and so
cheat them of shaded ways for rest and sport and love.

There also are the birds—the gentle martins,
swallows that will seem the perfect flower of the
home sweetness in stern cottages on the heights and
warm farmhouses in the valleys, the chiffchaffs that
shall sing in the ash and the larch, the delicate wrens
of the woodland crests and the tempestuous nightingales of the thick-budded copses, silent flycatchers
for the plum trees on southern walls, cuckoos to shout
over the dim water-meadows and in the pearly lichened
oak woods, ouzels to flash on the moors, skyey swifts,
doves to fill the green caverns of the beeches, and all
the chatterers that hide in blackthorn and cornel

thickets when it is best to walk among them; and the men heave, for they are coming to the land even now.

Very near now are the lizards of the drowsy nettle-beds, snakes to curl and uncurl upon the sunlit moss, and blue sylphs for the rivulets. All are coming in from this placid sea; and so the men heave, and the white houses begin to glitter, and the golden mist over the sea promises that days shall again be long, and men shall sit carelessly on gates and sleep under the hedge at noon, and adventure and make plans in the pure mornings that are at hand.

CHAPTER XLII

THE tide moves the river northward, towards me, under the bridge on which I stand. On both sides it is lined for a little way by houses; on the east in a flat, straight front, on the west in irregular rocky masses. Those on the east are coldly stained with light from the western sky; those opposite are vaguely shadowed and have an airiness and gloom—not a light yet appearing—as of the other side of Lethe. The river is of noble breadth.

Against the eastern houses rise up the masts of seven fishing boats in a row, with only such movement as makes the shadow run into the brown and gold, or the gold and brown into the shadow of the sails slowly, like the unfolding of poppies; and under their sides the shadows are profound, as if they trailed black velvet mantles that hid the water. For, away from the boats, the unrippled surface of the motionlessly gliding river is of that lugubrious silver that seems to be, not water, but some trick of light upon mere air, such as is seen above summer meadows in the heat.

And over all is bent a pale, soft, empurpled sky, and in it a crescent moon.

Up the river come two fishing boats, sleeping, their motion the only proof of the tide—no man visible on board—no voices—and their sails of a colour as if they had been steeped in the early hues of the now vanished sunset, and yet in their folds so dark that they seem to be bringing with them the night as a cargo from those cloudy black woods in the south. Beyond the large curve of those woods the shining horn of the river reaches the unseen sea. The spirit of the sea comes up on the broad silent water.

The two small, solemn boats still glide in sleep; the others dream at the quay.

Southward, the dark wood sends out the narcotic night as a gift over the land, sowing the seeds of it from the wings of the slow sea birds, from the two incoming boats, silently; and now they have fallen upon good soil in the seven boats on the quay, in the masses of houses, in the arches of the bridge and in the hearts of men, and all things drink oblivion. As I turn away there is a sound of shrill, passionless voices that may be the souls of the oblivious travelling to content somewhere in the rich purple night.

CHAPTER XLIII

CLOUDS OVER THE SEA

THE high, partridge-coloured heathland rolls southward, with small ridges as of a sea broken by cross-
winds, or as if the heather and the hard gorse cushions
had grown over ruins which time had not yet smoothed
into the right curves of perfect death. A gentle wind
changes the grass from silver to green, from green to
silver, by depressing or lifting up the blades. In the
dry heather and pallid herbage the wind sounds all
the stops of despair. The note that each produces is
faint, and the combination hardly louder than the
sound that fancy makes among the tombs. Nevertheless, the enchantment of that little noise pours into
the ear and heart a sympathy with the thousand
microscopic sorrows and uncertainties of the inanimate
world—a feeling that is part of the melancholy im-
portunately intruding on a day of early spring. The
larks rise, linking earth and sky with their songs,
and the stonechats are restless.

There are no trees. The only house is a little,
white, thatched cottage among some shining dark
boats, on the distant rosy shore.

The sea makes no sound. It changes with the sky
so often and so subtly that its variations are to be
described, if at all, in terms not of colour but of
thought. All such moods as pass through the mind
of a lonely man, during long hours in a place where
the outside world does not disturb him and he lives

on memory and pure reflection, are symbolized by those changes on the surface of the sea. Now it is one thing and now another; the growth is imperceptible and those moods that have passed are as hard to reconstruct as the links of a long, fluctuating reverie. For the most part it is grey, a grey full of meditation and discontent.

The heathland changes with the sea. Both take their thoughts and fancies from the sky. For this is a world of clouds; earth and sea are made by them what they are. They make the sea, and they make the little pools, blue, silver, or grey, among the gorse. The clouds are always there; inhabiting a dome that is about fifty miles from the horizon up and down to the opposite horizon; and yet they are never the same.

Where do the clouds go?

The large white clouds, mountainous and of alabaster and with looks of everlastingness. I see them in the north at midday, making the hills seem level with the plain. I turn away my eyes and when next I look they are gone. They vanish like childish things. One day I made an appointment with another child to play marbles on the next morning; I never went; I forgot; I never saw the boy again, and I remember it now, for I never played marbles after that.

The high white halcyons of summer skies.

The distant, icy ranges of rounded pearl down which, in terrace after terrace, the sun walks like a king to the sea in May. As I watch they grow big like roses in the sun, and they change and vanish and reappear beneath the restless sculptor's hand. If a man loves what is passing away, he loves then.

Those little dove-like clouds that for a moment

stain the dusky clouds after an April storm—are they
a metamorphosis of the Pleiades? They are gone like
music; for sometimes the memory of them equals the
reality and sometimes they are not to be recalled.

Those Elysian, white sierras in the east, which, at
the end of a day of frowns and humours, stretch far
away in still and lucid air, their bases lost in blue,
making the world immense, as if it were to be thus
for ever and the gods to walk again.

The cliffs that hold the moon imprisoned in their
clefts and lure the mind to desire useless things.

The flocks that go down into the sea or behind
the mountains, and thrill the heart with adventurous-
ness and yet never move it to an adventure, but rather
persuade us to care greatly for nothing except to muse
and mesmerize ourselves with that old song:

> I did but see her passing by
> And yet I love her till I die.

The parcels of aerial gold which at sunset make one
canopy as of a golden-foliaged tree planted over the
world. The night does not believe that they were
ever there.

Those caravans that go down the blue precipices
of night intently; those dragons, lean and black, that
prepare the dawn and ruin the morning star.

They change, they tarry, they travel far, they pass
away, they dissolve, they cannot die. Up there, do
they think, or do they watch, or do they simply act?
and is it pleasant simply to act? Have all the sunsets
and dawns and thunderstorms done nothing for them?
I suppose that up there also nothing matters but
eternity; that up there also they know nothing of
eternity.

CHAPTER XLIV

THE MARSH

THE sun has gone down. Except on one hand, the immense empty marshland expands to the sea, and where it mingles with the grey water would be uncertain, but for the clamour of the wading birds and the gleam, now and then, of a white wing. The low bent thorns, inland, now take on a strange humanity, as of men who have ventured out into the solitude and pitched their tents there and none has followed them; they are bent in alarmed and hurrying attitudes away from the sea, but cannot leave it. The sea rises steeply up like a vast ploughed field to an uncertain sky of the same hue. All that greyness takes hold upon the mind like autumn rain and lures it to we know not what desperate carelessness; and the siren, that sweet evil of the sea, chants such dissolving melodies as this:

> The woods of Arcady are dead,
> And over is their antique joy;
> Of old the world on dreaming fed;
> Grey Truth is now her painted toy;
> Yet still she turns her restless head;
> But O, sick children of the world,
> Of all the many changing things
> In dreary dancing past us whirled,
> To the cracked tune that Chronos sings,

Words alone are certain good.
Where are now the warring kings,
Word be-mockers?—By the Rood,
Where are now the warring kings?
An idle word is now their glory,
By the stammering schoolboy said,
Reading some entangled story:
The kings of the old time are fled.
The wandering earth herself may be
Only a sudden, flaming word,
In clanging space a moment heard,
Troubling the endless reverie . . .

But at one hand lies the first house in the world, a little ark of grey stone, pierced by windows behind which a velvet darkness weaves a spell and by a gloomy doorway; knock there and at once you will be barricaded again against the annihilating sea and night. All about it a trim garden of white and gold and dying red sends up a thin tower of scent that stands bravely in the salt wind. A tower!—at such an hour, when the casements of all the senses are opened wide upon eternity, this perfume not only satisfies the desiring and aspiring sense, but, with all its unsearched, undiscovered powers, builds for us here upon the shore a specular tower and, more, a palace lovely and shadowy, where the mind roves slowly and at ease, saluting vaguely apprehended shapes, rinding now long lost memories of men and things which time has locked against a thousand keys, and now bold hopes and unexpected consolations. Content herself lurks here and many a pleasant ghost that seems immortal because it has died many times, and they may be enjoyed, until suddenly the night wind, without mercy, overturns the tower and desolates the palace and leaves us forsaken. Yonder the lighthouse flashes. The ships go

out with wings as of a moth that cannot leave its
chrysalis behind. The church bells moan; the sea
birds whimper and shriek, and the road that goes on
so long as we can walk lengthens out along the marsh
and up the hill.

CHAPTER XLV

ONE SAIL AT SEA

THIS is a simple world. On either hand the shore
sweeps out in a long curve and ends in a perpendicular,
ash-coloured cliff, carving the misty air as with a
hatchet-stroke. The shore is of tawny, terraced sand,
like hammered metal from the prints of the retreating
waves; and here and there a group of wildly carved
and tragic stones—*unde homines nati, durum genus*—such
as must have been those stones from which Deucalion
made the stony race of men to arise. Up over the
sand, and among these stones the water slides in
tracery like May blossom or silver mail. A little way
out, the long wave lifts itself up laboriously into a
shadowy cliff, nods proudly and crumbles, vain and
swift, into a thousand sparks of foam. Far out the
desolate, ridgy leagues vibrate and murmur with an
unintelligible voice, not less intelligible than when one
man says, "I believe," or another man, "I love," or
another, "I am your friend." Almost at the horizon
a sharp white sail sways, invisibly controlled. In a
minute it does not move; in half an hour it has
moved. It fascinates and becomes the image of the
watcher's hopes, as when in some tranquil grief we
wait, with faint curiosity and sad foretelling, to see
how our plans will travel, smiling a little even when
they stray or stop, because we have foretold it. Will
the sail sink? Will it take wing into the sky? Will
it go straight and far, and overcome and celebrate its

success? But it only fades away, and presently another is there unasked, yet not surprising, and it also fades away, and the night has come, and still the sea speaks with tongues. In the moonlight one strange flower glistens, white as a campanula, like a sweet-pea in shape—the bleached thigh-bone of a rat—and we forget the rest.

CHAPTER XLVI

THE castle stands high among vast, sharp-edged waves
of sand at the edge of a cliff, and looks at the sea
and a long, empty shore. At its feet a little river
can be seen running in a narrow valley. A few miles
off it rises in the red moorland, then it falls with
many a cascade down ladders of crag, broadens among
willows where long leaves are all horizontal in the
wind, and here by the castle it has reached an elvish,
merry old age already, as it moves clear over the
brown stones and out among the rocks to the sea.
Opposite the castle, across the river, the other side
of the valley is clothed in dense and luminous oak
wood. Where the river joins the sea both the castle
hill and the wooded hill break away into a broken
multitude of bristling rocks, and among their alleys
and hidden corridors and halls the waves leap with
the motion of a herd of ridgy cattle galloping through
narrow gateways. Beyond, and away for ten miles,
the high dark coast sweeps in a curve which the sea
whitens by showing its teeth; and round the headland
at the end the ships come and go at starry intervals.
Landward, the country rises in long, steep, furzy
curves, interrupted by sudden rocks, to the red moor
and the autumn evening sky of towering, tumultuous,
and yet steady grey cloud.
The castle stands among pale sand and long plumy
grasses. The sand is deep within the hollow and
roofless circuit of the broken walls, through which,

here and there, come glimpses of sea or sky disconnected from any fragment of the land, so that I seem
to stand between the sea and sky. In the summer
ivy-leaved toad-flax buds, and harebells, most delicate
flowers, whisper from the crevices. But nothing lives
here now. The trunk of an old tree that once grew
through the walls is now so much worn that what it
was when it lived is not to be known. Not only is
all human life gone from here, but even the signs of
its decay are invisible. The noble masonry can suffer
no more except at the hands of men; it is too low and
too strong. It is a rude crag. Neither history nor legend
speaks intelligently of it. It is but known that it was
raised by hands, and each man that comes to it has to
build it again out of his own life and blood, or it remains
not far removed from nothing. The wayfarer starts
at the sight of it, tries in vain, shuddering at the
cliff and the desolate sea, to conceive a life lived by
beings like himself in such a place. To have lived
there men must have had fairy aids or the blood of
witches or of gods in their veins.

Here might easily have been builded in a night that
phantom palace and its illusive pomps, where the
Corinthian Lycius dwelt with the phantasmal Lamia
until a philosopher's eye unbuilt it again.

Or on these sands might have stood Myratana and
blind Tiriel before the beautiful palace, and cursed
their sons.

Or up in the vanished high bowman's window the
king's daughter sat and harped and sang:

> There sits a bird i' my father's garden,
> An' O! but she sings sweet!
> I hope to live an' see the day
> When wi' my love I'll meet.

When the sun has set, and land and sea are dissolved in cold mist, all but a circle of pale sand and the castlè fragment, it seems true that here, to the foot of the tower that is gone, came the king's daughter and wept and sighed and made a great moan: "Ah! he mourns not who does not mourn for love." And the good king came and asked her if she desired to wed, and she answered, "Alas, sire, yes. Ah! he mourns not who does not mourn for love."

> Las! il n'a nul mal qui n'a le mal d'amour:
> Las! il n'a nul mal qui n'a le mal d'amour.
>   La fille du roi est au pied de la tour,
>   Qui pleure et soupire et mene grand dolour.
> Las! il n'a nul mal qui n'a le mal d'amour:
> Las! il n'a nul mal qui n'a le mal d'amour.
>   Le bon roi lui dit: Ma fille, qu'avez vous?
>   Voulez-vous un mari? Hélas! oui, mon seignoux.
> Las! il n'a nul mal qui n'a le mal d'amour:
> Las! il n'a nul mal qui n'a le mal d'amour.

Here, away from earth and sea and sky, apart from men and time and any care, the melody and the picture are truer than before, suiting that melancholy wood, in which the heart, seeming to go back easily through unguessed deeps of time, makes all sorrows its own, airily, not without delight.

And there are others who abode here or abide here, as for example those timeless knights of no age or clime—Pelleas, Launcelot, Pellinore, Palomides, Galahad, whose armour no man pretends to show us, whom old men's tongues and poets' pens have lured into immortality—to whom this castle gives a home.

When Launcelot had come to the water of Morteise, says Malory, he slept, and there in a vision he was bidden to rise and put on his armour and enter the first ship that he found. And he did so, and the ship moved without sail or oar, and in the ship was great sweetness so that "he was fulfilled with all things that he thought on or desired." There he slept, and when he awoke there was none on board except the dead sister of Sir Percivale; and the ship went on for more than a month and Sir Launcelot fed on manna, until at last he touched land and there met Sir Galahad, his son. For half a year the two sailed together, and "often they arrived in isles far from folk, where there repaired none but wild beasts." But one day at the edge of a forest a white knight warned Sir Galahad that he should stay with his father no more. "And therewith Galahad entered into the forest. And the wind arose, and drove Launcelot more than a month throughout the sea, where he slept but little, but prayed to God that he might see some tidings of the Sangreal. So it befell on a night, at midnight, he arrived afore a castle, on the back side, which was rich and fair, and there was a postern opened toward the sea, and was open without any keeping, save two lions kept the entry; and the moon shone clear. Anon Sir Launcelot heard a voice that said: Launcelot, go out of this ship and enter into the castle, where thou shalt see a great part of thy desire. Then he ran to his arms, and so armed him, and so went to the gate and saw the lions. Then set he hand to his sword and drew it. Then there came a dwarf suddenly, and smote him on the arm so sore that the sword fell out of his hand. Then heard he a voice say: O man of evil faith and poor belief, wherefore trowest thou more on thy harness than in thy Maker, for He might more avail thee than thine armour, in whose service thou art set.

Then said Launcelot: Fair Father Jesu Christ, I thank Thee of Thy great mercy that Thou reprovest me of my misdeed; now see I well that ye hold me for your servant. Then took he again his sword and put it up in his sheath, and made a cross in his forehead, and came to the lions, and they made semblaunt to do him harm. Notwithstanding he passed by them without hurt, and entered into the castle to the chief fortress, and there were they all at rest. Then Launcelot entered in so armed, for he found no gate nor door but it was open. And at last he found a chamber whereof the door was shut, and he set his hand thereto to have opened it, but he might not.

"Then he enforced him mickle to undo the door. Then he listened and heard a voice which sung so sweetly that it seemed none earthly thing; and him thought the voice said: Joy and honour be to the Father of Heaven. Then Launcelot kneeled down before the chamber, for well wist he that there was the Sangreal within that chamber. Then said he: Fair sweet Father, Jesu Christ, if ever I did thing that pleased Thee, Lord, for Thy pity ne have me not in despite for my foule sins done aforetime, and that Thou show me something of that I seek. And with that he saw the chamber door open, and there came out a great clearness, that the house was as bright as all the torches of the world had been there. So came he to the chamber door and would have entered. And anon a voice said to him: Flee, Launcelot, and enter not, for thou oughtest not to do it; and if thou enter thou shalt forthink it. Then he withdrew him aback right heavy. Then looked he up in the middle of the chamber, and saw a table of

silver, and the Holy Vessel, covered with red samite
and many angels about it, whereof one held a candle
of wax burning, and the other held a cross and the
ornaments of an altar. And before the Holy Vessel
he saw a good man clothed as a priest. And it
seemed that he was at the sacring of the mass. And
it seemed to Launcelot that above the priest's hands
were three men, whereof the two put the youngest
by likeness between the priest's hands; and so he lift
it up right high, and it seemed to show so to the
people. And then Launcelot marvelled not a little,
for him thought the priest was so greatly charged of
the figure that him seemed that he should fall to the
earth. And when he saw none about him that would
help him, then came he to the door a great pace,
and said: Fair Father Jesu Christ, ne take it for no
sin though I help the good man which hath great
need of help. Right so entered he into the chamber,
and came toward the table of silver; and when he
came nigh he felt a breath, that him thought it was
intermeddled with fire, which smote him so sore in
the visage that him thought it brent his visage; and
therewith he fell to the earth and had no power to
arise; so he was so araged, that had lost the power
of his body, and his hearing, and his seeing. Then
felt he many hands about him, which took him up
and bare him out of the chamber door, without any
amending of his swoon, and left him there, seeming
dead to all people. So upon the morrow when it was
fair day they within were arisen, and found Launcelot
lying afore the chamber door. All they marvelled
how that he came in, and so they looked upon him,
and felt his pulse to wit whether there were any life
in him; and so they found life in him, but he might

not stand nor stir no member that he had. And so they took him by every part of the body, and bare him into a chamber, and laid him in a rich bed, far from all folk; and so he lay four days. Then the one said he was alive, and the other said, nay. In the name of God, said an old man, for I do you verily to wit he is not dead, but he is so full of life as the mightiest of you all; and therefore I counsel you that he be well kept till God send him life again.

"In such manner they kept Launcelot four-and-twenty days and all so many nights, that ever he lay still as a dead man; and at the twenty-fifth day befell him after midday that he opened his eyes, and when he saw folk he made great sorrow, and said: Why have ye awaked me, for I was more at ease than I am now. O Jesu Christ, who might be so blessed that might see openly thy great marvels of secretness there where no sinner may be! What have ye seen? said they about him. I have seen, said he, so great marvels that no tongue may tell, and more than any heart can think, and had not my son been here afore me I had seen much more. Then they told him how he had lain there four-and-twenty days and nights. Then him thought it was punishment for the four-and-twenty years that he had been a sinner, wherefore our Lord put him in penance four-and-twenty days and nights. Then looked Sir Launcelot afore him, and saw the hair which he had borne nigh a year, for that he forthought him right much that he had broken his promise unto the hermit, which he had avowed to do. Then they asked how it stood with him. Forsooth, said he, I am whole of body, thanked be Our Lord; therefore, sirs, for God's love tell me where I am. Then said they all that he was in the Castle of Carbonek."

And when the moon is clear, and the tingling sea is vast and alone, this castle on the sand above the grim coast is Carbonek, meet for all adventures and all dreams.

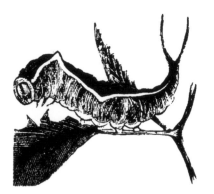

SONGS

MOWING SONG

With one man, with two men, we mow the hay to-gether;____ With three men, with four men, we mow the hay to-ge-ther.____ My four, my three, my two, my one no more____ We mow the hay and rake the hay and car-ry it a-way to-ge-ther.

THE HOLM BANK HUNTING SONG

One morning last winter to Holm bank there came A brave, noble sportsman, Squire Sands was his name, Came a-hunting the fox, bold Reynard must die, And he

THE HEART OF ENGLAND

flung out his train and be - gan for to cry, Tal - ly ho! ___ tal - ly

ho! ___ Hark, for - ward a - way, tal - ly ho! ___

POOR OLD HORSE

My cloth - ing was once of the lin - set wool - sey

fine, ___ My tail it grew at length, my

coat did like - wise shine. But now I'm grow - ing old my

beau - ty does de - cay. My mas - ter frowns up - on me; one

day I heard him say, Poor old horse, poor old horse.

MARY, COME INTO THE FIELD

Ma - ry, come in - to the field, To work a - long of
I _____ Dig - ging up man - gel wor - zels For
they be a - grow - ing high Dig 'em up by the
roots, _____ dig 'em up by the roots, _____ Put in your spade
don't be a - fraid, Dig 'em up by the roots. _____

LA FILLE DU ROI

Las! Il n'a nul mal qui n'a le mal d'a - mour!
Las! Il n'a nul mal qui n'a le mal d'a - mour! La
fille du roi est au pied de la tour, qui pleure et sou-

227

pire   et   mène   grand dou - lour   Las!   Il   n'a

nul   mal qui n'a le mal d'a - mour   Las!   Il   n'a

nul mal qui n'a le mal   d'a - mour   Le bon   roi lui   dit :_____ 'Ma

fille, qu'avez - vous?   Vou - lez   vous un mari?' 'Hélas, oui, mon siegn - oux!'

Las!   Il n'a   nul   mai qui   n'a le mal   d'a - mour!

Las!   Il n'a   nul   mai qui   n'a le mal   d'a - mour!

228

Printed in Great Britain
by Amazon

34082680R00142